Additional Praise

"In our industry, leadership and mentorship have always been very important for career success. By sharing their stories in this inspirational book, these women demonstrate the many paths to leadership and the mentoring help they had along the way. They encourage all of us to persevere on our journeys, not just for ourselves but for those who follow."

   — **Bobbie Kilberg,** *President and CEO, Northern Virginia Technology Council (NVTC)*

"I've always believed in the power of women lifting up other women, sharing their wisdom and rules for success. When you read this book, you'll hear the voices of the women as if you were interviewing them yourself, and their stories will inspire you."

   — **Kathleen Matthews,** *Executive Vice President, Marriott International, Former News Reporter and Anchor, WJLA-TV*

"Reading these stories helped me remember that the lessons I've learned from other women gave me the best guidance for my own path to success. Having diverse perspectives around the leadership table not only makes sense from a cultural perspective—it is critical to technological innovation and business success as well."

   — **Cynthia Good,** *editor and CEO of PINK magazine and of the daily e-Note "Little PINK Book"*

"A group of remarkable individuals—who happen to be women— share the stories of their lives and the lessons they have learned. By gathering and publishing these stories, WIT created a valuable resource for both men and women."

   — **Anne Armstrong,** *President, 1105 Government Information Group*

"Realizing one's greatest potential as a leader is not a one-time event but rather a series of lifetime experiences and events and a demonstrated level of commitment to learn. *No One Path* is a wonderful guide to learning practical insights, techniques, and wisdom for up-and-coming women in technology who are looking at furthering their career aspirations. *No One Path* contains excellent real-life examples of how senior women leaders in technology focused on the right actions to take their leadership to the next level."

    — **Rebecca Shambaugh,** *President and CEO, SHAMBAUGH Leadership; Founder, Women in Leadership and Learning;, Author,* It's Not a Glass Ceiling, It's a Sticky Floor

"*No One Path* captures the life stories and lessons of forty-eight remarkable women in a compelling, up-close-and-personal way. While each has unique experiences and insights, the similarities among their stories are striking. Without exception, the leaders profiled in this book are responsible risk takers who are authentic, optimistic, and courageous. Their wise and practical advice speaks to all of us."

    — **Ralph W. Shrader, Ph.D.,** *Chairman and CEO, Booz Allen Hamilton*

"The path to leadership is not one that you can learn from a textbook. Rather it is guided by the stories of those who come before us—the collection in this book is just that. Throughout, there are unique insights that will help all aspiring leaders blaze their own trail."

    — **Ted Davies,** *President, Unisys Federal Systems, Unisys Corporation*

"This book is about women who have worked hard in technical industries and defined success for themselves. As you read this book, think about the education, competence, and character of each woman conveying her story. These three aspects of your life establish and define your reputation. If this book helps you learn about the importance of education, competence, and character, you have learned well."

    — **Leslie F. Kenne, LtGen,** *USAF (retired)*

"The inspirational stories of these extraordinary women are a must-read not only for females in technical fields, but for anyone looking for a healthy dose of motivation. It will become a classic reference for all of us who aspire to great things."
   — **Mary-Claire Burick,** *President, MC Strategy Inc.*

"The stories in this book show us that a leader needs to have FOCUS...and that focus must be on the right target. There are twists and turns in life that can draw our attention away. Sometimes this can be for self-preservation and sometimes this can be because of concerns about our own performance in the present. In this book, each of these women inspires us to greatness by remaining focused on what matters most to her despite the twists and turns she encounters along her leadership journey."
   — **Linda Cureton,** *CIO, NASA Goddard Space Flight Center*

"A marvelous collection of life stories demonstrating that leadership in the technology arena, and in reality anywhere, can be achieved via many and diverse paths."
   — **Joanne Woytek,** *NASA SEWP Program Manager*

"Inspirational words for any leader or leader in the making. This should be required reading for every young woman. Look to these pages for stories of integrity, achievement, balance, encouragement—and for wonderful examples of what we can be when we 'grow up.'"
   — **Renee Winsky,** *President and Executive Director, Maryland Technology Development Corporation (TEDCO)*

"Women's inspiration is unique, and inspired women have no limits. As mothers, daughters, sisters, wives, and industry and community leaders, women need to share with each other in order to learn from each other. No matter what the story is, there is always a message that touches someone. *No One Path* provides the stories of women leaders throughout Washington DC—each with her own journey and wisdom. This book is a wonderful source of inspiration from which we can all learn and in turn inspire others around us."

    — **Vicki Kirkbride,** *CEO and Executive Director, The Women's Center*

"Throughout my career, I have valued my WIT affiliation because it offers an extraordinary assembly of successful and accomplished women. The stories in this book inspire me and, I hope, will inspire my students as they launch their professional lives."

    — **Jill A. Klein,** *Information Technology Executive in Residence, Kogod School of Business, American University.*

"Fifteen years ago the idea of bringing women together to learn about emerging technologies and to network was a long shot. Little did we know the pent-up need for this type of forum. As we celebrate WIT's fifteenth anniversary and the tenth year of the Women in Technology Leadership Awards Program, we see the power of women leaders to leverage technology to achieve success. Congratulations to all and thank you for sharing your stories with us."

    — **Valerie W. Perlowitz,** *Founding President of Women in Technology*

No One Path

Perspectives on Leadership from a Decade
of Women in Technology Award Winners

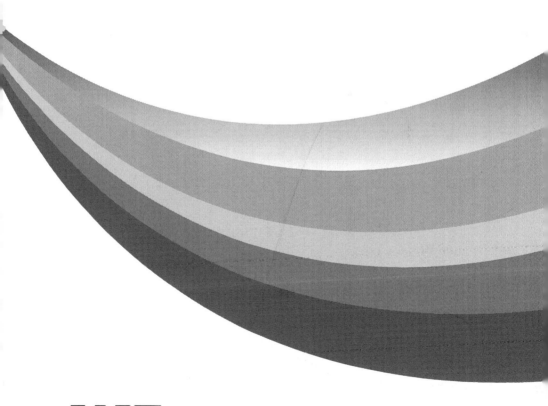

WOMEN IN TECHNOLOGY
Connect. Lead. Succeed.

No One Path

Path

Perspectives on Leadership from a Decade
of Women in Technology Award Winners

10378 Democracy Lane, Suite A
Fairfax, VA 22030
Phone: 703-683-4003
www.womenintechnology.org

Design by Paras Productions, Inc.
Printed in the United States of America

Library of Congress Control Number: 2009908705

ISBN: 1-4392-4500-2
ISBN-13: 9781439245002

Dedication

For the women in this book
and all they inspire

Contents

Preface

Writing a book is no easy task under the best of circumstances. Would writing this book, inspired by Maureen Bunyan's urging to tell the amazing stories of these women leaders, even be possible, relying as we were on a group of volunteers?

The answer—Yes! In November 2008 the "Bunyan Book" committee held its first meeting. Twenty volunteers showed up. During the following eleven months WIT volunteers undertook the process of writing and publishing the book. Researchers, interviewers, editors, and marketers donated their time and effort. The committee surged to more than fifty members. The WIT Leadership from other committees offered support and ideas. And every step of the way the WIT Board demonstrated its commitment to the initiative—funding the project, making critical decisions, and offering guidance.

As WIT marks the ten-year anniversary of the Leadership Awards and the fifteenth anniversary of WIT, the organization is proud to present this compilation of perspectives on leadership from the past winners of the WIT Leadership Awards, including a foreword by Ms. Bunyan. (For more information on the criteria for award selection, please see Appendix B.) Forty-eight women share their views on what makes a good leader, their most difficult challenges, who helped them along the way, what advice they would give to aspiring women leaders, and the legacy they'd like to leave behind. Each journey is personal, each woman's story shaped by the situations, people, and opportunities she encountered as she found a way to become the author of the next chapter in her career.

Women in Technology's tag line is Connect. Lead. Succeed. Sharing lessons learned about mentorship and leadership, and recognizing women who excel, are central to this organization. Our hope is that this book will inspire women and girls to pursue their goals in science, technology, engineering, and math; continue to honor the women WIT has recognized over the years with the WIT Leadership Awards; encourage companies to grow and advance the women in their ranks; and raise awareness about Women in Technology.

Enjoy.

Foreword

I should have grown up to be an electrical engineer, a biochemist, or a computer analyst, according to my father's plans for me.

Arthur Bunyan loved technology and all things scientific and mathematical. In our home in southeastern Wisconsin, he turned one bedroom into his laboratory, filled with oscilloscopes and other instruments that buzzed and glowed. Many evenings and weekend afternoons, I sat next to him, dozing off more than once, as he explained the principles of electricity and tried to teach me how to use a slide rule.

But while he was curious about how "things" worked, I was more curious about how "people" and the institutions they created worked. My interests led me to journalism and news broadcasting.

In the spring of 2008, I served as the emcee for the annual awards program of Women in Technology held in McLean, Virginia.

As I read the introductions for the women who were being honored, I was struck by their amazing stories, including their willingness to serve as leaders in their fields.

Suddenly, the journalist in me felt compelled to say to the audience, you must tell the stories of these amazing women...you should write a book! Yes, that's it...a book! It would inspire young women to go into science and technology careers. You could sell it and raise funds for scholarships and it would show the world how far women have come in these fields! Yes, ladies...you can do it! (Applause, applause!)

Fast forward (as we say in broadcasting) to January 2009. I received a phone call from Charlotte Pelliccia and Sue Liblong, past and current WIT presidents. They asked, "Do you remember that idea about the book you mentioned last year?"

Yes, I said.

"Well, we're going to do it. As a matter of fact, we formed a committee and we're well underway. We hope to have it published by the end of the year! And the working title is The Bunyan Book!"

I knew the women of WIT were highly focused and organized, but they were also extraordinarily busy people with serious professional and personal responsibilities. How would they find the time, to say nothing of the motivation, to produce a book?

What a silly question!

What you will find in the following pages is the response to that question. It is a response that will inform you, entertain you, and impress you. These are the stories of women honored by WIT, how they supported each other and how they have become leaders in their communities and how they came to excel in science and technology, fields dominated by men.

The women in this book are part of a tradition that goes against the grain of Western culture. It was about a hundred years ago that women began to break the cultural and legal barriers to their education in science and engineering. But even before that, women always used their common sense and natural talents to contribute to technological development. Is there any doubt that women in primitive societies designed and created agricultural implements such a digging sticks, hoes, and simple plows? Or that women developed the tools and processes to store perishable foods, to weave cloth and dye and sew garments, and to create herbal medicines and other remedies?

Today, women still struggle against prejudice that keeps them from getting the best education in science and technology. But, as these women show you in this book, their struggles dim in the light of their accomplishments.

I may not have grown up to be the engineer or scientist my dad wanted me to be, but I did grow up to understand how important it is to tell the stories of people's lives. I think Arthur Bunyan would have been proud to have known these women who achieved so much in the fields he loved. And I think he would also have been pleased that his daughter had something to do with telling their stories.

—Maureen Bunyan
Primary News Anchor at WJLA-TV (ABC 7) and Winner of Seven Local Emmys
July 2009

Chapter 1

What Makes a Good Leader?

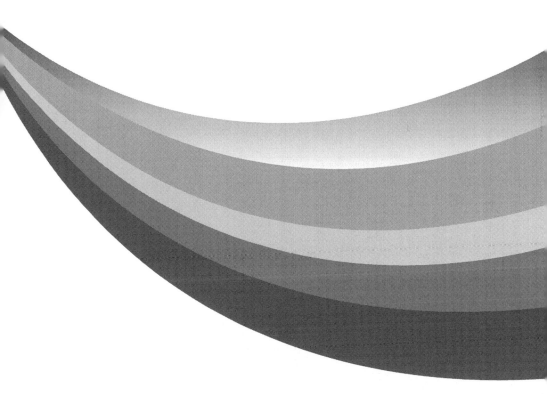

DEB ALDERSON
Putting Power in the People

by Cindy Lancaster

Crafting her own leadership skills from the examples set by her mother, her graduate school advisor, and her first professional career supervisor, Deborah Alderson learned early in life that caring for people and confidence in being able to accomplish anything were the two things that would drive her own success. These two guiding principles have motivated and inspired her throughout her career, and have resulted in amazing success: first-line vice-president of Techmatics, Inc., and member of its Board of Directors; senior vice-president and leader of the Systems Engineering Group when Techmatics was acquired by Anteon; and corporate executive for all Anteon support to the Department of Homeland Security.

Today, as the president of SAIC's Defense Solutions Group, Alderson oversees a team of more than 12,000 professionals that generates more than $3 billion in revenue annually. She is also the executive sponsor for the Women's Network, an employee group which grew from 800 to 2000 members under her leadership, and executive sponsor of SAIC's multicultural network. She is the only executive to sponsor two employee initiatives of this type.

Here, Alderson, winner of the 2007 WIT Corporate Award, shares what she's learned about leadership—from her mother, her mentors, and her own experience.

A People-Centric Perspective

Alderson was one of three children of a young widow. "My mother took adversity head-on, would not give up," she said. "She focused on taking care of the family; she was a true survivor." One of the qualities Alderson admired was her mother's caring and appreciation for all people. "Even when we didn't have much, I can't remember a Christmas without someone less fortunate sharing our home and table," Alderson recalled. "She just wouldn't have it any other way."

Alderson applies that same people-centric perspective to her employees today. "You have to focus on people," Alderson said. All people inherently want to do a good job, she believes. "It's the responsibility of a good leader to put people in a position to succeed and excel."

In her graduate studies at Virginia Tech, the drive and focus of her advisor, Dr. Enid Tozier, reinforced the lessons from her mother. And, Alderson said, "[Dr. Tozier] taught me I could accomplish anything I wanted to." Alderson has done just that, from her early days in the professional services industry in 1983 as a systems analyst at Advanced Technology, Inc., to her current role at SAIC.

Some of the biggest flaws we see in leaders show when they forget to treat people as individuals.

Her professional mentor, Adm. Meyer, also reinforced the message that taking care of people was the most important action for a leader, and that a good leader takes time to put them in the best position to succeed. "He was always reaching out to people," Alderson said. "He would sponsor events for military families, reach out to others in industry, always trying to touch the lives of as many people as he could."

Emotional Intelligence and Collaboration

As important as technical skills and knowledge are in today's contracting world, Alderson feels that the "soft skills" are still some of the most important for leadership success. "I don't think you can be an effective leader without those," she said. "Some of the biggest flaws we see in leaders show when they forget to treat people as individuals. Edicts don't work. People react differently and hear messages differently."

Leadership that encourages collaboration is key. "It's not top down, not bottom up; it is all collaborative," Alderson said. A key element of collaboration resides in information sharing and knowledge—and unfortunately, many times leaders hoard information or use it to demonstrate their power. "I don't use information as power," she said. "I want everyone to know everything!"

Alderson's leadership style transforms the use of information as power. "I am always using it to move everyone in the same direction," she said.

Good Character

Given the extraordinary leadership positions Alderson has achieved in her career, one might wonder what she looks for in other leaders. The people-first thread again surfaces: "Focus on the people around you, have a willingness to take risks, and be open to changing direction," she said, and added that often leaders who make a bad decision aren't willing to admit it or change. On the other hand, when good leaders make bad decisions, she said, "... they have a willingness to change their minds. They are able to respond to external forces and outside data and adjust; they are open to other views, can change course, and can say to people 'I made the wrong decision.'"

Alderson also believes that good leadership is a combination of character and strategy. And like Marla Ozarowski (see p. 23), she believes that if you have to be without one of the pair, be without the strategy. "You're nothing without character," she said. "You can buy strategy."

BETTY ARBUCKLE
Good Leaders Jump In, Nurture Talent

by Patricia Crew

Perhaps the best way to describe Betty Arbuckle's leadership style is simply to say this: she jumps in whenever and wherever necessary to bring about critical results. She is quick to take up a worthy cause and see it through to a successful conclusion. In the process, she's enhanced her leadership skills and developed a clear philosophy of what it means to be a good leader.

Making a contribution to society is Arbuckle's ultimate concern, and she has taken on the mantle of leadership in her career and in her personal life. As of this writing, Arbuckle, who won the 2002 WIT Founders' Award, is a principal with Washington Financial Group, where she generates value-added consultative sales of insurance products, retirement services, and life-planning services. Her tag line reads "Lifetime Strategies for Lifetime Clients." Even though Arbuckle has a full-time career and is the mother of three boys, she finds time to volunteer at the zoo and to lend her leadership skills to a number of professional organizations such as Women in Technology (WIT), the Association for Corporate Growth, and the Estate Planning Council.

In the early years of WIT, Arbuckle was instrumental in beginning and implementing the first Mentor–Protégé Program. When the designated program chair suddenly became ill, Arbuckle was quick to step up and make the program happen.

In her work with the Association for Corporate Growth, an organization for executives focused on bringing value to their organizations, Arbuckle accepted responsibility for chairing its sponsorship program. "I wanted to be taken seriously so I took on a very difficult role in [bringing in] sponsorship," she says. "I chose [committee volunteers by identifying] people ... who had connections and were experts in their field." Her efforts paid off: she brought significant sponsors into the association.

"When you are in leadership, you jump in without hesitation and just do things," Arbuckle says. But she acknowledges that leadership isn't just a matter of "just doing it."

"A good leader quietly puts the spotlight on the people around [her]," she explains. "[A good leader] is willing to hear others, makes others feel good about themselves, validates others, creates trust and gives up control, has a way of making people want to do whatever is at hand, participates fully with others on the project, and is nurturing to others and self."

Arbuckle believes that character is integral to leadership. "Integrity, honesty, straightforwardness, and being even-handed are all central," she says.

She also believes that one of the most important and often the most difficult aspects of leadership may be emotional detachment. "It is important to stay emotionally detached as a leader in the midst of controversy, to listen to what others have to say," Arbuckle says, "... and in short, to utilize emotional intelligence."

A good leader quietly puts the spotlight on the people around [her].

Leadership doesn't happen in a vacuum, of course—being a leader implies knowing how to work with those who are charged with helping the leader achieve her goals. So Arbuckle never short-changes the process of selecting staff. On any given project or initiative, she intentionally identifies and selects the most competent and connected people to help her achieve her goals.

"I bring in people who have specific project area expertise," Arbuckle says. "Pulling in experts provides the energy to make a project happen and be successful."

She is not intimidated by intelligent, knowledgeable, and competent people. Rather, Arbuckle says she is able to nurture a person's "native" talents—and, she adds, "... to utilize relationship cultivation, advocacy skills, and political strategy"—to achieve goals and to get a program in place.

ANNE-MARIE HARTLAUB-KESSEG
Maintaining a Delicate Balance

Loyce —
You made this
possible! Many
thanks Anne-marie

by Loyce Best Pailen

Retired Navy Captain Anne-marie Hartlaub-Kesseg, recipient of the Women in Technology 2005 Government Award, easily describes her perspectives on good leadership and the qualities that define it. Her tranquil waterfront home on Beards Creek in Maryland provided an intimate setting for sharing her thoughts on what makes a good leader, including glimpses into her own career in the Navy and the Pentagon, her insights about leadership's defining moments, and advice for would-be leaders.

What Makes for Good Leadership

Hartlaub-Kesseg posits that leadership consists of baseline qualities combined with special characteristics.

The basics, of course, are education, professional experience, and common sense. Hartlaub-Kesseg's undergraduate degree in computer science and master's degree in statistical analysis give her the technical knowledge she needs to be a leader in information technology. Professional experience and common sense come to the forefront in the human side of leadership: being able to work well with others, knowing how to react in special situations, empowering and praising workers, being sensitive to an individual's concerns, possessing passion and conviction with the ability to articulate both—even understanding the subtle messages conveyed through body language. Essentially, she says you should be "tuned in" to those around you to respond best to their needs and yours.

Yet as a successful woman in male-dominated careers, Hartlaub-Kesseg has honed her skills in compartmentalizing issues, analysis, and problem solving—skills she attributes mostly to male leaders. "I've been fortunate to be exposed to effective leadership examples throughout my career," she says, "retaining the good leadership tools and dumping the bad ones."

One of the good ones is her focus on people, following the wisdom of Rear Admiral Grace Murray Hopper, a leading computer scientist and pioneer, who said, "You manage things; you lead people."

Hartlaub-Kesseg attributes her success to maintaining the delicate balance between getting the job done and caring about the people with whom she works. She strives to create a trusting environment for both superiors and subordinates where they can think and act with integrity, and always seeks ways to make everyone look good and to accomplish the mission.

Her own career in the Navy, and later in the Pentagon, is an example of putting these qualities in action.

Synopsis of a Career

Excellence, success, and leadership in the eyes of men and women alike define Hartlaub-Kesseg's Navy career. She was the first woman officer aboard the USS Simon Lake (AS-33) to qualify as Engineering Officer of the Watch, and she earned her surface warfare designation in only thirteen months. During her tenure in Simon Lake, she helped the ship earn the coveted "Red DC" award for Damage Control Excellence. Hartlaub-Kesseg championed the development and implementation of a technologically advanced awards system, the Navy Department Awards Web Service, launched in March 2004. She followed this with the Navy Organization Request Management System, which tracks Navy organization changes via the Web. These achievements were recognized as contributing to the nation's efforts to fight terrorism.

Hartlaub-Kesseg retired from the United States Navy after twenty-four years of active duty and in April 2007 returned to the Pentagon as a federal civil servant in the role of Deputy Director of the Department of Defense Continuous Process Improvement/Lean Six Sigma Program Office. As a recently certified Lean Six Sigma Black Belt, Hartlaub-Kesseg continues to sharpen her professional skills and never rests on her laurels. Her colleagues describe her as an exemplary role model and visionary leader.

Leadership's Defining Moments

Hartlaub-Kesseg recognizes that it's sometimes the moments that make—or break—a leader. For her, those leadership moments include taking risks and stepping mentally and physically outside traditional boundaries. For instance, she applauds President Obama's groundbreaking speech to the Muslim world in Cairo,

Egypt. "It took courage for the President to take a different international turn [to] try to heal a rift," she says, "and to empower others, who may stereotype Americans, to see us as human beings—just as they are."

Hartlaub-Kesseg herself has had such moments. Recently, for example, she stood up in front of 700 of her peers for "the right thing to do" regarding advice to the White House and the Office of Management and Budget about running an effective continuous process improvement (CPI) program. The right thing to do, she believes, is to share Department of Defense (DoD) knowledge in CPI across all federal agencies. This idea is controversial, but she feels good about the potential outcome—her ability to articulate ideas and deliver them with conviction led to successfully working through the challenge of linking CPI projects to DoD enterprise-level strategic goals and objectives, garnering support from peers and leaders.

There's no substitute for "doing the right thing."

Hartlaub-Kesseg's confidence, which is rooted in her long-standing ability to speak out, is tempered with the knowledge that it is perilous for leaders to think they are always right. Ego can be a dangerous thing; humility keeps it under control. This is where emotional intelligence becomes immensely important to effective leadership. Hartlaub-Kesseg strives to show appropriate humility, "owning up" to missteps, "picking your battles," "knowing your audience," and steering conversations appropriately in times of crisis.

Space for Reflecting, Recharging

Years of twelve-hour days devoted to ensuring the success of projects and people have taught Hartlaub-Kesseg the value of surrounding herself with all the amenities leaders need to decompress. At home, she and her husband, John, enjoy the environmental beauty and impeccable design of their waterfront home. Any visitor can see the love and labor they have put into creating an atmosphere where any leader could "recharge" and focus on the relationship-building skills that leaders need.

The Kessegs' house and grounds provide an intimate setting that allows the couple to either share or individually reflect on their thoughts—or merely bird watch and enjoy the beauty of Beards Creek. The Legion of Merit and the Meritorious Service Medal, along with many other awards and plaques, adorn Hartlaub-Kesseg's home office—one befitting a high achiever. "It's the first time I've had room to hang everything up on the wall!" she exclaims.

The Kessegs' "children," three beautiful Siamese cats named Captain Jack, Honey, and Admiral Sassy, provide affection beyond what one would expect from their species—so much so that the Kessegs often refer to them as "dogs in disguise." During the interview, in fact, Captain Jack insisted on greeting this author up close to relay acceptance into the "brood," while Admiral Sassy repeatedly dropped her favorite toy at Hartlaub-Kesseg's feet to be thrown and subsequently retrieved. Their animals' elegance and grace in movement only adds to the serenity that allows Hartlaub-Kesseg to focus on leading in the often hectic military and government environments in which she works. The ambience of her home provides the inspiration and balance she so often cites as necessary for leadership success.

Hartlaub-Kesseg is often approached by aspiring young women who wish to be like her "when they grow up." Her advice to them sums it all up:

- Get a good education—a master's degree is imperative.
- Push hard while you are young and have the energy.
- Build your career and experience the world before settling down with a family.
- Be the best at your work regardless of the task.
- Keep the bar high.
- Most of all, demonstrate integrity and be honest in all that you do. There's no substitute for "doing the right thing."

LEAH HOOTEN-CLARK
A Recipe for Great Leadership

by Ellen Quinn

When asked to describe her personality, Leah Hooten-Clark, recipient of the 2006 WIT Rising Star Award, turns to family history. As with any good family, there is a circuit of embarrassing stories that gets recited at yearly family functions. Hooten-Clark recalls the following story her mother tells about her youth.

At the age of three, Hooten-Clark was enrolled to attend preschool twice a week. After her fourth birthday, the frequency was increased to three days a week, and she decided that it was no longer acceptable to be taken to school by her mother. Because Hooten-Clark insisted on riding the bus like the older children, her mother paid extra to have the school bus pick her up and drop her off. At the end of each day, her mother greeted her at the corner where the bus had dropped her off. And every day, Hooten-Clark returned the greeting with a glare and demanded, "Why are you here? I don't need you here! I'm big enough to walk home by myself." She then stormed home in front of, not next to, her mother.

Hooten-Clark acknowledges that her "I'm ready to take on anything" personality has probably been her greatest strength, and sometimes her greatest weakness, throughout her life. Taking on new tasks, stretch assignments, and challenges has always come naturally to her.

One of Hooten-Clark's early challenges presented itself when she joined Northrop Grumman in 2001. Hooten-Clark initially took part in rotational assignments in test design engineering and international marketing, and then landed a permanent position in the group RF Power Systems. In 2004, Northrop Grumman awarded Hooten-Clark the Johns Hopkins University Part-Time Advanced Study Award, and in 2006, she earned a master's degree in systems engineering, graduating with honors.

Hooten-Clark's work in power systems began with detailed analyses of the power distribution network within transmit/receive (T/R) modules. Hooten-Clark was a member of a T/R module design team that received Northrop Grumman President's Leadership Award in 2002. She expanded into end-to-end power system analysis and eventually into the role of power system lead engineer. Today, Hooten-Clark leads the development of the power system for an advanced ground-based tactical radar system. She's also participated in the Leadership Development Program at Northrop Grumman, which cultivates growth through training and networking.

Throughout her career, Hooten-Clark has wanted to be well-known by senior management as a person who not only "gets the job done right" every time, but, just as importantly, as one whose team people seek to join. Possessing one or the other of the above characteristics is easy; encompassing both is the challenge.

One important characteristic of a leader is the ability to know when to stop and listen.

Mentors have often aided her in these pursuits. Her most influential mentors are people who have the ability to provide guidance even if she thinks it isn't needed. It is these people's generosity she knows she will never be able to repay. Through them, Hooten-Clark has learned that one important characteristic of a leader is the ability to know when to stop and listen.

Hooten-Clark also learned that one of the greatest leadership goals is self-awareness. Her message is to use awareness of one's own strengths and weaknesses, as well as those of one's team, as a guide in developing organizational strength. A significant component of being a tremendous leader, she believes, is being able to identify what is needed in one's organization compared to what one has, filling in the voids, and then moving the organization in a common direction.

Hooten-Clark takes inspiration from Theodore Roosevelt, who said, "The best executive is the one who has the sense enough to pick good men to do what he wants done, and self-restraint to keep from meddling with them while they do it." She has found that leadership involves surrounding oneself with people who possess skills that add to one's own, synergistically melding a diverse group of personalities and capabilities into an integrated team. Self-awareness, combined with the ability to create a strong team by choosing the right members, she believes, is the key to being a good leader. By adding vision and a dose of self-restraint, letting people do their tasks and delegating more to the team, the recipe for a great leader is complete.

TITI MCNEILL
Stoking that Fire in the Belly

by Kathy Albarado

After speaking to Titi McNeill, winner of the 2001 WIT Leadership Award, for just a few brief moments, one is drawn in by her energy, drive, and passion.

McNeill, winner of the 2001 WIT Leadership Award, is CEO of TranTech, an IT solutions and service provider that she founded in 1989 to serve the federal and commercial sectors. She is clearly dedicated to growing her business in order to provide ample opportunities for her employees, while at the same time ensuring that her clients' needs are addressed. Though she has done this successfully for nearly twenty years, she still says, "It's not enough. We can always do more!"

It is this passion for doing more that characterizes her own leadership style—and it is also what she admires in other leaders.

"You can recognize a good leader quickly," McNeill says without hesitation when asked what makes a strong leader. "She has energy and passion... a good leader will trust her managers and leadership team to do what is in the best interest of the company."

McNeill's personal philosophy is one of perseverance and optimism. She is always hopeful and believes she and her team can do anything.

"A [strong] leader knows what she wants and goes for it!" she says. "They dream of something big, talk big, and have the commitment to follow through. [They are] the people who do what it takes to get the job done. They make things happen."

Although this philosophy has served her well, McNeill also recognizes that it can be a potential danger zone. She has learned to balance her optimism with a realistic view of when it's time to stop placing energy and resources into a situation that may not actually be successful.

McNeill also believes that good leaders create an environment of trust and honesty—they are always authentic. "[A good leader always speaks the truth]—because you can't camouflage yourself and be a good leader," she says. Her honesty and directness extends to clients and employees alike. "I always say what I mean and mean what I say."

But honesty and directness alone are not enough, McNeill suggests. She strives to treat her employees with compassion and ensures that they know she cares about them personally. If you personally care about your team and make it clear that they can come to you with their issues and challenges, she believes, they will provide you with an opportunity to address a situation before it escalates beyond repair.

What advice would she give aspiring leaders? "If you have fire in your belly and really want to do something to make something happen...then don't let anyone talk you out of it," she says. In a nutshell, she recommends that aspiring leaders

- Set goals.
- Believe in themselves.
- Work hard.
- Stay awake to make it happen!
- Understand it may get rough, but not give up.
- Believe in what they're doing.

If you have fire in your belly and really want to do something to make something happen...then don't let anyone talk you out of it.

"If you're not moving forward," McNeill adds, "you're standing still. And then you die."

In my view, McNeill is a remarkable woman. Our interview left me energized with renewed optimism to step forward in meeting my own goals and continually challenging myself to stretch beyond my own comfort zone.

CAROL MOROZ
On Creating Safe Environments for Failure—and Success

by Lachelle McMillan

Ability to establish a vision, communicate it, and get people energized around it. Intellectual curiosity. Professional respect. Trustworthiness. Energy and dedication. These are some of the critical qualities that Carol Moroz, 2008 WIT Champion, believes define a great leader.

She shaped this definition as a result of having worked at different organizations, in different areas, and with various executives throughout her career. Early on, for example, Moroz worked at a technology company founded by an individual who had fostered a great culture and committed to establishing that culture in each of the company's global offices. Employees' good work was recognized and rewarded. In addition, employees at all levels experienced a sense of togetherness. For example, there was no reserved parking or special dining for executives, as the CEO did not want to create a sense of "arrogance" among the executives or a sense among employees that the executives were "removed" from what was happening in the workplace.

Though the leader had succeeded in energizing the employees around his vision, the company, unfortunately, later closed, partly because the founder failed to recognize that technology was evolving in a different direction than he had anticipated. This taught Moroz another lesson about good leadership—that a great leader should possess the following critical qualities:

- Ability to establish a support network that can provide different perspectives.
- Knowledge of your strengths—are you a visionary or executor?
- Intellectual curiosity that spurs you to challenge the possibilities and continue to ask, "What's next?"
- The ability to welcome innovative ideas and not feel threatened by those who suggest them.

- The willingness to find and hire people smarter than you are.

A great leader should also be unafraid to create an environment where people can fail. Sound strange? Not so much. Past experiences taught Moroz that failure is a great teacher. "You learn the most from failures," she says. "You cannot advance unless you have failed."

You learn the most from failures. You cannot advance unless you have failed.

People must feel empowered to experiment with different ideas and approaches to issues that surface in the marketplace. However, they won't take that chance if there are risks of being fired. Therefore, a great leader must create a supportive environment where new ideas are encouraged.

Moroz also knows that a great leader is often supported by a great team. Once, for example, she worked with a manager who knew how to pull the team together and earn trust from them all.

The ability to "foster team development and appreciate the unique qualities of each team member" is important, Moroz notes, emphasizing that there must be a commitment to the team succeeding. "[This means there is] no back-stabbing," she adds. "Team members are supported...brainstorming is welcomed...and everyone is treated professionally."

EVA NEUMANN
Essential Ingredients: Intuition and Decisiveness

by Martha J. Padgette

Awards and other artifacts of accomplishment and recognition splash the vibrant walls—accented in purple, orange, green, and blue—of the offices of ENC Marketing & Communications. ENC's founder and president, Eva Neumann, is no stranger to success—among other honors, she's received the 2000 and 2001 WIT President's Awards and the 2007 WIT Founders' Award. She acknowledges the struggles and lessons learned along the way, and some lessons, she assures, she is still learning.

Among top leaders, certain qualities and the lessons that forge them emerge as essential. This is true in the wisdom Neumann shared in our interview. The key traits in a good leader, according to Neumann, include a passion for quality and doing things well; the need for humor, compassion, and decisiveness; the willingness to stretch yourself beyond preconceived limitations; and, finally, the importance of recognizing and trusting your intuition.

It is this last trait, she admits, that is one of the most challenging—and one she says (only half-jokingly) that she is destined to repeat.

Going with Your Gut

Throughout her career and volunteer efforts, Neumann has possessed a strong passion for quality and been an impressive agent for change. But in order to bring these virtues forward, she had to learn several important lessons—one being that leaders must give credence to the value and validity of intuition and use it in decision making. "We cannot be afraid to 'go with our gut,'" she says.

Typically, when you go against your gut "you are fighting [it] because you don't want to do something... [that] you know is the right thing to do," Neumann says. Intuition is a valuable tool that can help greatly in making quick and sound decisions.

Being decisive as a leader is absolutely vital, Neumann further emphasizes; this is a common mantra among successful leaders. She becomes very passionate when underscoring that we cannot "be afraid to make a decision and live with [the results] or fix it." It is imperative that we not be afraid of making mistakes; that fear will become a road-block to progress or success. Neumann, on the other hand, reveals that "all of the mistakes I've made have shaped me."

And as a leader, you have to be able to create a compelling case as to why your decision is the right decision. "Your decision may be totally wrong," she adds, "...[many] leaders make bad decisions."

But is a bad decision necessarily a wrong decision? Neumann smiles and leans back before generously sharing some wisdom her father once imparted on decision making. "[He would say that] once you make a decision," she says, "you have made the best decision available at the time and you can't second guess it." That perspective is quite freeing because you've made the decision with the best knowledge and best intentions that you had.

Regardless of whether the decision is good or bad, Neumann believes that leaders cannot be afraid to have their decisions regarded as unpopular. "It is inherent in being a leader that your decisions are not always going to be popular," she says, "but you must have enough conviction, strength, and stamina to stay focused because you know it's the right thing to do."

Managing Change and Failure and Creating Success

Neumann is not only intuitive and decisive. She continually strives to figure out how things can be done better.

A need for something better was the catalyst that led Neumann to launch her own company. When she worked in high-tech companies, she experienced many frustrations when hiring advertising agencies and marketing firms, often having to provide training in government marketing for account executives and sometimes having to re-do their work. Establishing ENC and meeting customer needs brought a strong sense of satisfaction as she developed "something of quality to market ... providing the service or product that solves [a] challenge or business need."

As in any new venture, there were successes and challenges—and change that brought both difficulties and rewards. When Neumann speaks of these, her eyes brighten and her passion and energy rise. With pride, she shares an initially painful experience where she was confronted with a difficult situation resulting from a few bad hires.

The situation was threatening to erode the work environment.

She took immediate action, hiring a human resources company to help her understand what went wrong and how to avoid a similar situation in the future.

And she was very candid about it. "I know I'm going to make mistakes," she said, "but [I wanted to know] how do I minimize the chances of making a mistake in hiring, and how do we identify ... the right [hiring] questions to ask ... to ensure we minimize our risk?"

Neumann used the qualities defined during that effort to identify the type of person who would thrive and be successful in ENC's environment, and to help establish the company's core values and behaviors.

All of the mistakes I've made have shaped me.

This list of traits became a guidepost for the company and its employees, and it influenced performance evaluations. Neumann, through change management, introspection, and direct action, had taken an erosive situation, learned from the challenge and mistakes of the past, and used the subsequent jewels mined by the process to propel her company forward.

JEANNE O'KELLEY
Leader by Nature—or Nurture?

by Dianne Black

Jeanne O'Kelley was just nine months old when she took her first steps. Her mother recounts the story: "Jeanne learned to walk because I couldn't move fast enough for her." And O'Kelley, winner of the 2009 WIT Corporate Award, continued to move fast and show signs of a natural-born leader throughout her childhood as well as her professional career.

Seeing and Seizing Opportunities

O'Kelley has always been one to apply creative solutions whenever she perceived a need.

In 1968, for example, O'Kelley looked down Jefferson Road, where she lived in suburban Maryland, watched the neighborhood kids running around with their many activities, and exclaimed out loud, "We need a street newspaper!" O'Kelley then set out to publish the Jefferson News. She organized the neighborhood kids as reporters. "We need stories! Go find them!" she directed, and enlisted help from her parents to copy (on mimeograph) the newspaper for distribution to the neighborhood. The paper made a profit—five cents per copy. The successful venture revealed O'Kelley's natural tendency to see and seize opportunity and inspire others to realize her vision.

She did it again when she successfully raised money for muscular dystrophy—while still in grade school. The story? O'Kelley had been a huge fan of the comic book Archie. While reading one of the issues, she came upon an advertisement about individuals setting up carnivals to raise money for muscular dystrophy, a cause with which she was familiar because of Jerry Lewis' telethons. An idea began to percolate. She sent away for the information, organized a team of neighborhood kids to help, and staged the carnival. Naturally, it, too, was a success—as was a school-wide show, sponsored by

O'Kelly's middle school class government body and organized and produced by O'Kelly herself.

Never shy about taking on challenges, O'Kelly credits her "can do" attitude to her father. He always encouraged her, telling her there are no limits to what she could do.

Solving Problems, Making Tough Decisions

O'Kelley's "can do" attitude and desire to meet needs with creative solutions continued in her professional career. She had graduated from college when the first personal computers were coming out. As she began to learn about the PC, O'Kelley wondered, "How will it talk to other devices like video machines, computer game machines, and printers?" Thinking it was a basic necessity to solve the printer integration challenge, she started her own business, Integration Specialist, Inc. The business took off.

O'Kelley then started another company, Blueprint Technologies (now a subsidiary of Vangent). The company, which provided enterprise architecture solutions and services to government and commercial markets, won multiple Deloitte awards. In her view, the successes came from being focused, studying the market drivers, establishing a clear goal and vision, being committed to her team, and communicating her passion and drive about the business. Unfortunately, after 9/11, the economy shifted, and Blueprint Technologies lost eighty percent of its business.

I went back to the fundamentals of leadership: understand the environment, look for opportunities, focus on solutions, and most importantly, take it one day at a time.

It is a truism that great leaders emerge in such difficult times. O'Kelley found her own strength as a leader by going back to the fundamentals of leadership: understanding the environment, looking for opportunities, focusing on solutions, and most importantly, "taking it one day at a time." She had to lay off two-thirds of the staff. She then refocused the business and eventually sold it to the company she works for now.

Today, O'Kelley leads a life filled with passion, focus, and a continuing commitment to solve problems. As a mother she has witnessed the positive influence that these attributes have had on her daughter. Though young, her daughter demonstrates the same curiosity and passion to find creative solutions as her mother.

Considering her own leadership skills and those she sees emerging in her daughter, one wonders what she'd say if asked whether leaders are born or bred. Her answer? "Both."

MARLA OZAROWSKI
Listen. Inspire. Empower.

by Cathy Hubbs

Looking back at her career, 2005 WIT Champion Marla Ozarowski reflects that her first job exposed her to great leadership. She worked with an inspired and innovative team on a project she still regards as "the best." What made it so?

"The leadership," she said. They created a positive atmosphere, she explained: "The staff felt they could change the world, there was passion, and everyone believed we could make [it] happen."

Ozarowski remembers the CEO gathering the team together and saying, "To do the impossible, you must first believe it isn't." This first experience set the stage and opened Ozarowski's eyes to what makes a great leader. Later, throughout her career, Ozarowski was introduced to a variety of leadership styles. She learned that listening, integrity, and empathy are the pillars for the kind of balanced leadership that unites employees.

A less coveted quality, rarely proclaimed, is that great leaders don't always have the answers; they empower those around them, listen, and continue to move forward. Perhaps Robert Louis Stevenson said it best: "Keep your fears to yourself, but share your inspiration with others." The moral? Great leaders must have the confidence and strength to make decisions and provide direction even when the path is unclear or fraught with risk. Or when the path goes against conventional wisdom. In that case, according to James Callaghan, "A leader must have the courage to act against an expert's advice." Ozarowski's own experience echoes Callaghan's observation.

In the early 1990s, while working in the telecom industry, for example, Ozarowski was fortunate to witness great leadership in action.

"The team faced Q4 challenges to make revenue and profitability goals for the year. I remember thinking that the easy approach would have been to require longer hours," she said. "However, the leader declined to take that approach. Instead, he pulled fifty to sixty people off a billable project for a full day and took them offsite for a team-building experience at an athletic facility. There were morning meetings that encouraged open dialogue and inspired brainstorming. Together they looked for opportunities to work through the challenge they faced. In the afternoon, leisure activities were the focus and included games, relaxation, and sports. The team went back to the project re-energized and committed. The result? The profit goals were surpassed."

It is said leadership is a combination of character and strategy, and if you have to be without one, be without strategy. It's a view Ozarowski supports, and even embellishes: "While having character without strategy can weaken an organization," she notes, "having strategy without character can lead to failure."

I am there to support [my staff and employees], and in that sense I work for them.

Ozarowski further believes that emotional intelligence is strongly related to good leadership. "[Great leaders can create] a sense of purpose and mission, team and organizational identity, and a healthy sprinkling of excitement. It's all about how you treat people and the example you set for others," she said. "I have always taken the viewpoint that my role is to enable my staff and employees to excel. I provide them with vision and direction. I am there to support them, and in that sense I work for them."

Her view parallels John Gardner's, i.e., the idea that leaders can "articulate goals that lift people out of their petty preoccupations and unite them in pursuit of objectives worthy of their best efforts." It's also a concise description for the hallmark of leadership: listening with empathy, continually reflecting and reaching for higher self-awareness, being inspirational and supportive, and most importantly, giving back, which Ozarowski has done through her work with Girls in Technology. But that's another story.

CHARLOTTE PELLICCIA
Fueling Great Leadership through Relationships

by Pam Krulitz

Charlotte Pelliccia, past WIT President and recipient of the WIT 2006 Champion and 2007 and 2009 President's Awards, insists she is "NOT a touchy-feely person!" She has a results-focused style, a history of success at multiple companies where she has held high-ranking positions such as senior VP of marketing, and now her own successful marketing consulting practice since 2003. However, despite Pelliccia's own beliefs about her leadership style, when asked to describe the characteristics of outstanding leaders, she praises those who are "charismatic," "mesmerizing," and "give you tingles." When Pelliccia shares the moments she's witnessed great leadership, she offers examples that sound more raw and vulnerable than metric-driven and determined. Nevertheless, her observations indicate that seeking out excellent leaders and identifying the qualities that make them great has been an important part of Pelliccia's own journey to leadership.

Pelliccia has been a student of leaders throughout her career. She laughs as she recalls the "messes she made managing people" early in her career when her leadership approach consisted of "reading the task list for [her staff]." When a couple of staff members rebelled, Pelliccia realized that she had been overly focused on tasks and narrow-minded in her view that everything had to be done her way. She began to wonder: "How do you get [your staff] excited about what you [need] them to do?" And with that, Pelliccia's career began to become a journey of successes, each gradually helping to answer this question.

Pelliccia has continually sought and attained opportunities where she could learn from others. The importance of finding a company that provided more than a place to exercise her skills, for instance, was an important discovery. She gravitated toward companies that aligned with her values, provided opportunities to learn, and captured her heart as well as her mind. And these, she realized, were typically headed by leaders who possessed that rare ability to truly inspire others. They had invested themselves personally in the cause of their company and they wanted others to share their passion.

Relationships go a long way [toward] getting tasks accomplished.

Pelliccia's face lights up, almost with reverence, when she recalls those leaders who taught her the most about superior leadership. For example, when she was in her thirties, she learned much from a CEO with whom she worked at a software company. Though the company had had great success in developing and selling a novel product, what drew her to the company and kept her engaged was not the product, but the type of company they were creating together. There, Pelliccia felt like she was part of something important— something bigger than herself.

"It was more than just work," she said. This CEO conveyed a tremendous sense of commitment to the 200 employees and their families, and they responded with tremendous loyalty.

One moment stands out more clearly than the rest. It happened after the company had gone through a period of growth and the CEO recognized that many staff didn't know the company's history. As he told the story at a company-wide meeting, the CEO choked up while recalling where they had come from and the pride he had in what they had accomplished.

"Everyone was moved," Pelliccia recalled. "We were all just astounded that we were part of it."

She learned through this experience that showing emotion was not only permissible for a leader, but could be inspiring as well. Pelliccia's updated view on leadership style and success is that being smart and knowledgeable (aspects of one's IQ) is the "foot in the door"; however, one's EIQ (emotional intelligence quotient) may be the true determiner of one's broader success as a leader.

Now, Pelliccia understands that letting go of the focus on tasks and allowing others to make contributions is also part of encouraging people to become excited about what you need them to do. Great leaders, she believes, create an environment where all can share their ideas. Employees then "[envision] themselves as stewards," she says. "Their job is to help the company grow, not to have complete ownership over all ideas."

Pelliccia acknowledges that it all may sound a bit "soft"; however, she has learned over time that "relationships go a long way [toward] getting tasks accomplished." It is the fuel that gets things done. Pelliccia's experience is that the relationships created through the soft stuff are what get you through the hard times and allow you to reach the good times. And she has witnessed inspiring leaders create profitable companies that generated great wealth for many people.

Pelliccia aspires to emulate the inspirational leaders she has known. The traits she values in these exceptional leaders include looking for ways to help others do what they do best, showing appropriate emotion, being of service, and capturing people's hearts as well as their minds. Many who have worked with Pelliccia would say that she has already become a very inspirational leader herself!

GAYLE SWEENEY
Intelligence, Honesty, Commitment...
What Great Leaders Are Made Of

by Nancy Rawles

Like many other WIT award winners, 2009 WIT Champion Gayle Sweeney feels fortunate in having had good role models and opportunities to learn about leadership. And she took advantage of those opportunities. "I'm like a sponge, always ready to absorb new information," she says. She always wants to hear and learn more.

Sweeney began leading projects early. At AT&T, for example, she was able to lead projects in her first six months there. "[My first project] was for a configuration management system and it felt like trial by fire," she says, "yet it gave me the chance to learn and grow."

For a long time the AT&T project was the peak experience to which nothing else compared—a fun experience where she learned a lot about managing teams and discovered an innate desire to grow and lead people. Sweeney, keen to understand what makes a good leader and how to recognize one, continued to follow a career track that provided her with the answers.

The Most Important Qualities

Sweeney was very thoughtful in identifying the three most important qualities in the best leaders she knows: intelligence or intellectual capacity, honesty, and commitment.

Intelligence—a key prerequisite for competing in the high-tech and consulting fields—is what drew Sweeney to these fields in the first place. "I was always drawn to the sciences and solving new problems," she says. "I wanted to think, 'Yeah, how can I solve that?'"

As for honesty, the best leaders don't have hidden agendas, place blame, or dodge the tough issues. Sweeney found it easy to tell the best leaders she worked for what was going right and what wasn't, without being afraid of bringing forth bad news. When a project or idea failed, the best leaders took responsibility.

Responsibility goes hand in hand with a personal commitment to the organization. Leaders who have this kind of commitment know and are passionate about their businesses, and "the numbers" testify to their success.

How the Best Leaders Lead

In the best leaders, Sweeney believes, commitment encompasses not only building the organization, but also being committed to the people supporting it, and to society as a whole, not just to what the leaders themselves can cash out of it. In fact, great leadership takes a strong mastery of self. Great leaders must have the ability to remain committed to the achievement of the goals and detached from how or why to navigate through the challenges of the day-to-day business of driving the strategy. They can't take things personally.

But great leaders don't distance themselves from the people with whom they work. They balance a focus on tasks with an emphasis on connecting to and building relationships with the people with whom they work. In Sweeney's experience, the best leaders were those who had a good understanding of the tasks necessary to the job or business, but who didn't get bogged down in them. Less successful leaders tried to manage tasks and details and tried to cheerlead, but didn't understand the business sufficiently to know what was going on.

The difference between good leaders and great leaders is that great leaders don't get caught up in themselves.

Sweeney has come to appreciate some of the softer skills, like emotional intelligence, that are part of effective leadership. "It takes a strong sense of yourself [to remain focused] when everything else is going crazy around you," she says. "The difference between good leaders and great leaders is that great leaders don't get caught up in themselves."

Instead, great leaders ensure that their employees are empowered, are learning, and have creative opportunities; they are not micromanagers. Sweeney, though, doesn't get caught in the trap of "hands-off management vs. micromanagement." Instead, she believes, "[Good leadership] is a balance of the two."

Sweeney thrived best under leaders who gave her latitude and feedback, not directives. "There are people who want to learn and succeed, and need a lot of room to do that," she says. Great leaders give those people space.

A willingness to take risks is another hallmark of great leadership—and Sweeney has personally witnessed such moments in leaders she's known. One CEO with whom she'd worked, for example, had made a significant investment to go into an unproven Internet business. There were no certainties of a payoff—and he leapt into the void anyway.

"It was in that [kind of a] vacuum that great leadership is required," she says. "It comes from a willingness to take risks." This particular CEO had many businesses; some failed and many were successful. But the CEO was always willing to take a new chance.

Finally, great leaders create culture; they know it doesn't just happen on its own. They infuse their environment with energy and provide space for the people to be bigger or better than they ever thought they could be. This is the greatest gift that leaders can give their people, the space to accomplish something that seems impossible, to be able to say, "Wow, we made it here. Who would have thought?"

Intelligence, honesty, commitment.....after asking Gayle Sweeney to describe what great leaders are made of, it's hard not to come to the conclusion that she is also describing herself.

CATHERINE SZPINDOR
Don't Be Afraid of What the Future Holds

by Page Bostic

Catherine Szpindor, recipient of the 2005 WIT Corporate Award, has learned over the years not be
afraid of what the future holds. Not to be afraid to
take a chance in a new position, role, or location,
and to be willing to explore something different.
Her challenges have come in being committed to
the contributions of one's success, she admits—to
the continued persistence it takes to move forward
with innovative ideas that impact one's industry, and to develop the
qualities one needs to be a good leader.

The Longest Journey, A Single Step

When Szpindor started her career at an electrical gas company,
she had never seen a computer before. But she focused on the goal
of building her IT skills, and it was just the right fit, taking her from
that company to work at Nextel and finally to being vice-president
of IT at Virginia's Thomas Nelson Community College.

After that first success as a programmer librarian, Szpindor
wanted to learn more and take on more responsibilities, all while
watching what others were doing. "If they can do it, then I can do
it," she'd repeat as she continued to influence her managers in each
new position she secured. The phrase became her mantra, and as
she progressed her mantra evolved—"I want to do this and I can do
this," she'd tell her manager—always putting herself and her job on
the line to take on the next challenge.

Szpindor learned early that you have to build your "business
case" for what you are trying to do. It is gaining the buy-in and respect for what you are trying to accomplish that is most important
to her as a leader.

"Get everyone on board," she says. "Not until you do, can you
truly be successful."

Szpindor credits three qualities with enabling her to be a successful leader: understanding, patience, and compassion. But, Szpindor explains, it does not stop there: a leader must also be intelligent, and keep pushing in the direction of what she believes, making sure what she is pushing comes to fruition.

Yet the real test of a leader, according to Szpindor, is when things go wrong. "Helping a team through the bad period, and turning it around and being successful, can be a learning process that you can be proud of," she says.

"Doing" Leadership

How does Szpindor "do" leadership? She selects and develops people she can believe in—people who are responsible and committed to the job at hand. Szpindor believes that leaders cannot be successful without good people who work for them.

"You need to care about the people who you work with, the ones who work for you, and the ones you work for," she says. "Care by being understanding and by caring about them as people."

Get everyone on board. Not until you do can you truly be successful.

Staying committed to the decisions you make—from the smallest to the ones that can make or break your career—is another key component of leading well. Never be afraid to make the hard decisions. "Understand all of the alternatives that you have," Szpindor recommends, "and make the best decisions with the information that you have at the time."

Then it's time for action: "Do what you say," she states, "and say what you do."

When challenges arise, Szpindor addresses them by taking a positive attitude. She coaches her team to take a step back and adopt an analytical approach by breaking the challenge into smaller pieces and determining the best course of action. She tells her team that every day that they are in a position to impact technology, they are a "salesperson" in their respective fields.

"You have to figure how to gain support from those who are not in agreement with you and are preventing you from accomplishing your goals," Szpindor says. "You have to present your idea in such a way that they understand the benefit to themselves and to the organization. You have to deliver your message to build their confidence in you and believe that you can do what you say can do."

The View Ahead

Szpindor's crystal ball says that the future for women driving technology is "limitless." Women have a tremendous amount of potential for moving technology forward, she believes. She thinks that there is work that needs to be done to elevate women with technology backgrounds to the executive ranks in businesses. She would like to encourage more women to pursue technology careers, and young girls to develop math and science skills and embrace the industry.

"As technology changes, it's a wonderful time for us to look at it as a solution for education and healthcare," she says, "and it's a great time to be part of this industry."

LYDIA THOMAS
The Art of Leadership

by Pam Krulitz

During her thirty-six-year career, Lydia Thomas, the former president and CEO of Noblis and 2005 WIT Lifetime Achievement Award winner, has given quite a bit of thought to what makes a great leader. She believes that many people can learn and grow their way into being good leaders, but that there are a select few to whom leadership is innate—just as some people who play the piano for years become accomplished based on their hard work and practice, and others who are born true artists or prodigies make their gift look effortless.

Thomas would say there are very few "artists" out there as leaders—the ones who have it in their soul. "Being in their presence," she says, "is almost like being in the presence of genius."

For those mere mortals who have to work at becoming good leaders, every day is an opportunity to learn. Thomas says that the day she completed her doctorate in cell biology, she was thinking about pursuing a law degree. The practicality of earning a living trumped earning another degree, but Thomas' commitment to life-long learning and self-improvement continued. As she says, "Until the day you die, every day you have the opportunity to learn more. That's the journey that you're on....you're never finished."

Thomas' interest in learning about leadership from others started early in her career, when she began noticing those with whom she liked to work and why. She discerned the traits she admired, and believes it's important to observe other people to see what qualities and character traits set people apart. Role models may as likely be teachers, ministers, moms, or teammates as corporate executives.

But, she adds, observing others is only the first step. Equally important is being honest with yourself about whether or not you have those leadership qualities. As Thomas progressed in her career, she began to turn the mirror toward herself and wonder if and why people wanted to work with her. She has an aversion to the notion of leadership as simply a matter of skills training, applying the next two-minute solution, or getting the next promotion.

Based on her observations about leaders she admired, Thomas suggests first and foremost that great leaders listen and recognize completely that they don't know everything. When real leaders don't know something, they don't make stuff up. "The world is far too complicated a place," she says, "for anyone to be all and know all."

In Thomas' first management job, for example, her expertise in cell biology was only one of thirty-seven disciplines represented on her multidisciplinary team. It quickly became clear to her that listening to others was going to be paramount to the team's success. In her experience, difficult technical problems can only be solved through a combination of expertise in many fields, including science, engineering, and economics. The corollary to her belief that great leaders listen well and consider many views is that they also know when to stop listening and make a decision.

The second quality that makes the artists stand out from the paint-by-numbers practitioners in the leadership world is that they are believable. About one of the leaders she admires most, the former Chairman of the Noblis board of trustees, General Edward "Shy" Meyer, she says, "Whenever he says something to you, you don't have to wonder why he said it... That's the person you want to follow." She believes that it's critical for leaders to be honest—whether the news is bad or good.

The world is far too complicated a place for anyone to be all and know all.

She also notes that true leaders are able to connect with people individually. "They never forget people are people," Thomas says. When they're at the front of a meeting espousing the latest corporate strategy, she explains, they're aware that the people who are listening may have parents who are sick, or may be worrying about a child getting home from school or how they're going to send their kids to college.

"It's not like people walk in the door to work and all of a sudden become some automaton that can cut itself off from everything that makes it whoever it is," she says. "Real leaders never forget that." Thomas seems to have that kind of connection with people who work with her, easily calling them "Sweetpea" with genuine authenticity and respect when they drop by to ask a question or offer a comment.

In addition to General Meyer, her father stands out as another role model of a natural-born leader. As a high school principal during the integration riots in the South, he was able to gain the support of all races and bring the community together because the community believed in him. One would have to believe that he may have passed a bit of that leadership genius on to his daughter as well.

ROSE WANG
Leadership: A Two-Sided Coin

by Page Bostic

Rose Wang, recipient of the 2007 WIT Entrepreneur Award, built a successful award-winning business and became an entrepreneur by intention. After working for a large firm for thirty days when it bought out the start-up software firm she had worked for in Silicon Valley in 1996, she chose the path of independent contractor, quickly realizing that she had a desire to take destiny into her own hands. After launching two start-up companies that "failed spectacularly," Wang re-launched her company, Binary Group, with a new business plan in August 2000. Today she is Binary's CEO.

One of Wang's "secrets of leadership" was not being everything to everyone. When Binary first started operating, it was a typical small business in the government contracting sector. "You would do anything to make a dollar to survive," she says.

Once she realized her company had begun to "look and sound like everyone in the market," Wang reorganized her company to "IT Advisory," focusing on helping government organizations make better decisions and policy, and assisting with IT strategic planning, enterprise architecture, and project management.

"We limited one hundred percent of the pie to ten percent of the pie," Wang says. This was not done without hardship—Binary had to divest two contracts on the system integration side (and find jobs for a dozen people overnight) to stay pure to its model—but it set her business apart from her competitors' businesses.

Wang is passionate about learning, and incorporates it into her philosophy of good leadership. Her parents had always had a thirst for knowledge and modeled continuous learning, instilling this in her. Consequently, Wang defines herself as a leader who is always learning and believes that good leaders need to be open to new ideas, new ways of solving problems, and new perspectives.

The "Binarians" who work for Wang say that she is warm, makes tough decisions, is continually learning, and constantly looks for opportunities to connect the dots. "Our business is helping customers see better ways of solving problems, [make] better decisions... making sure we add value," Wang says. "In our heart of hearts, we felt that the market was going this direction and [by] staying pure, we would be more focused and attract more opportunities."

Good leaders need to be open to new ideas, new ways of solving problems, and new perspectives.

Wang strives to model the leadership qualities she feels are important: savvy, compassion, emotional intelligence, and the ability to empathize with others. The office environment—both the physical and psychological spaces—seem reflective of her intentions to cultivate a culture based on five core values: integrity, respect, creativity, responsibility, and excellence. People seem happy. Doors are open, employees are collaborating with each other. You'll frequently see them wheeling a big Smart Board into a conference room to work together, perhaps inspired by the display of Chinese poems and calligraphed characters of people Wang admires, and the expansive view of Georgetown University.

At the start of internal meetings, her team usually picks one of the values as a focal point for discussion. They read the value out loud and talk about who demonstrated that value, and how to further demonstrate it in the workplace. The values—rather than strict technical competencies—serve as the underpinnings of interactions within the company and the company's relationships with customers.

Not that competencies aren't important—they are. Yet, as Wang points out, "It doesn't matter how good you are at doing something... if you don't know how to deliver it to [those who] need to receive the information, you are not going to be effective."

Wang looks at leadership in a holistic way, seeing personal and professional leadership as intertwined. She's learned that in any leadership situation, it's ultimately the person as a whole in and outside of business who shows up. Wang illustrates this point using the metaphor of a coin. No two sides of a coin are the same, she points out. By standing the coin on its edge, however, one can see both sides.

"People call it balance, some call it [being] centered," Wang says. "If you create an open, creative environment, the opposite side is the fostering of that environment yet being disciplined enough to move in a direction while keeping that openness."

Chapter 2

Journeys, Challenges, Mentors

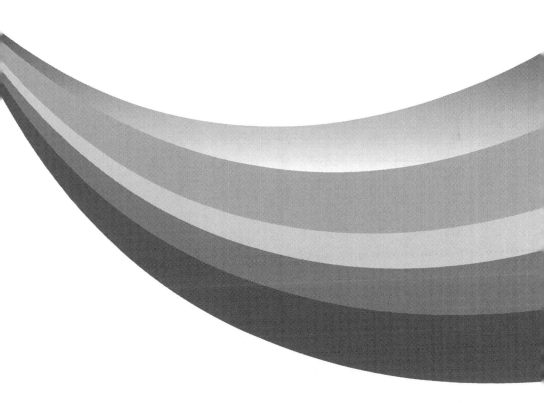

AMY BIELSKI
Challenge? Bring It On...

by Nancy Rawles

Amy Bielski, 2004 WIT Rising Star, thrives in a world of challenge. It started when she was young and had her biggest personal challenge, childhood leukemia, and continues today as she leads her own business. The name of her company, Ripple Effect, describes her well— that is exactly what Amy produces as she strides through life. She creates a wonderful ripple effect on her family, her community, her customers, and her employees.

Proving Herself

Learning has always been one of the biggest keys to Bielski's success. Her early career was extraordinarily challenging: she was a woman entering the information technology (IT) field in the early 1990s. When she first started working, ninety percent of her direct reports, peers, and bosses had IT experience. So she was always in situations where she had to prove her IT knowledge and gain credibility. The IT staff would tell her that what she was trying to do with the system "could not be done." But she persisted, and quickly discovered that the technology did exist and it "could be done." Her strategy? Keep asking questions until she learned and got it right.

At times, age got in her way. Not everyone had an equal respect for her capabilities; they thought she couldn't do what she claimed because she wasn't old enough. But again, she learned and got it right, so right that Bielski became the youngest person ever promoted to vice-president at the SHS division of ORC Macro, thanks to an extremely supportive leader, mentor, and boss who believed in her. Now, as president of her own business, Bielski deliberately hires people who disagree with her, to keep her balanced. And she hires people who are different from her, because she learned that success requires many different approaches.

Succeeding at Success

Broad-based learning is always a big part of Bielski's formula for success, whether success meant getting her MBA while she was a VP at Macro, or learning to paint pottery last year, or learning how to decorate a cake and taking financial classes while building her own business.

Listening is a large part of how Bielski learns. She feels fortunate to have had many people more senior than she take her under their wing and give her different perspectives on how to handle things. Those mentoring relationships are a recurring theme for her; they worked so well, she thinks, "because I really listen." Bielski is confident, not intimidated by someone more senior, however respectfully appreciative she is of their knowledge and what she is able to learn from them.

A very important contribution to Bielski's success, by her own admission, is a very supportive husband. Bielski and her husband have been married for eleven years. He stayed at home with their two daughters for the first five to six years of their lives so that she could continue to pursue her career. "Lots of husbands can't handle that," she says.

Having daughters makes Bielski very interested in supporting women's initiatives in the future. When her daughters were little they would play house, and the daughter who played at being the mother always went off with the briefcase; the daughter who played the husband stayed home. Wonder where they got that from?

Quitting was never really an option.

Facing Challenges

Bielski has faced and learned from challenges all her life. When she had childhood leukemia, she remembers being denied many opportunities from sixth through ninth grades—for example, she was prevented from being editor-in-chief of the yearbook. People were just trying to take care of her at the time, she explains, but she didn't see it that way. Instead, she felt she was being denied an opportunity.

When Bielski got to college she felt like she had a clean slate: no one knew her or was afraid she couldn't handle something. Later in life her parents revealed how much they had worried about her, but they told her that she was always so driven and nothing would stop her. Now that she is a parent she understands that so much more and can't even imagine what her parents went through during those times.

Her most recent professional challenge was the twelve to eighteen months of launching her new business, which she calls the painful year. It was a time when she didn't know where the next payroll was coming from. She had underestimated how much time, money, and strife it would take to pull off a new business. In addition she was grappling with her identity—shifting from being a "star employee" to being "just me." The turning point came when she hired a staff that would support her and help in areas that were not her strong suit—for example, finance—so she could concentrate on marketing and business development, which she did well.

And Bielski worked extremely hard. Not surprisingly, as difficult as it seemed at times, quitting was never really an option.

"Personally I exceeded my expectations. When I went for my MBA I expected to graduate," Bielski says. "But I didn't expect to have my own business. It taught me I can persevere through anything."

Starting with a vision of how a successful business of the future should be structured, Bielski realized that fast, high-quality computers are key to attracting and retaining talent in today's marketplace. Today's workforce demands adequate access to technology of all kinds. Bielski believes that today's workforce talent is made up of lifelong learners who want to constantly broaden their experiences and knowledge.

"At Ripple Effect we do not believe in extravagant offices, corporate bureaucracies, professional managers (who only manage and do not work), bloated executive salaries, country club memberships, fancy limos, corporate jets, or seats on the fifty-yard line," Bielski says.

So she is starting with her own clean slate and building her workforce of the future from the ground up. Right now she has twelve employees, owns two companies, and uses eight consultants. She wants to grow to one hundred employees over the next few years. Bielski faces the challenges of expanding at a rapid pace, growing infrastructure and processes, but she is keeping true to her vision, holding the reins while making sure no one is left behind, and learning "it's all in a day's work."

NIKOLE COLLINS-PURI
Seeing Beyond Challenges

by Maria Sanders

She listens to hip hop, attends Beyoncé concerts, and likes Will Smith movies. She grew up in a middle-class neighborhood in New Jersey, went to college, and landed a corporate job. Sound like your typical twenty-something life? Take a closer look and you'll realize that Nikole Collins-Puri, recipient of the 2008 WIT Rising Star Award, is anything but typical.

In the small town where she grew up, Collins-Puri was one of a handful of African-Americans and the only one in her high school. Many of the residents had never met an African-American before. She could have felt this to be a burden, a responsibility that weighed a bit heavy on the shoulders of a young woman her age. Instead, she saw it as an opportunity to represent her race, her family, and her community—and relished the challenge.

"I realized that leadership was sometimes just a matter of seeing things from a different perspective—looking at challenges and seeing them as possibilities rather than barriers," says Collins-Puri. "It has become the quiet voice of purpose within me."

It doesn't hurt that she has the work ethic to turn ordinary situations into extraordinary results. During college, she not only received a full athletic scholarship to the University of South Florida, but also managed to graduate with honors, while serving as senate president of the student government. In a day when her Generation Y peers might not expect to stay in a job or career for too long, she demonstrates employee loyalty that is a throwback to another era. She has been with her first and only employer, AT&T, for seven years. During her tenure, she's managed a Digital Subscriber Line (DSL) call center in India and worked with the operations group in Hong Kong to improve system efficiencies. Today, she heads up all diversity and inclusion initiatives for the Business Solutions Organization, a group with more than 60,000 employees worldwide.

"Leadership requires an ability to motivate, inspire, and influence those around you," Collins-Puri says. When she volunteered to lead her company's United Way Employee Campaign in 2006, she was able to "motivate, inspire, and influence" thirty-five hundred employees to donate $4 million in contributions and exceed the corporate goal by 110 percent. It's this same enthusiasm she channels into her volunteer efforts, mentoring young women in her community.

I realized that leadership was sometimes just a matter of seeing things from a different perspective—looking at challenges and seeing them as possibilities rather than barriers.

No matter the goal—even the intention (to become president of the United States) her nine-year-old self announced to her mother over a bowl of Cheerios—Collins-Puri has never once doubted she could do anything she put her mind to. Although the desire to be president is no longer there, what's left is the longing to help and serve her community and leave behind a legacy for the next generation.

If her first twenty-nine years are an example of Nikole Collins-Puri's future life's accomplishments, there is no doubt of her achieving that goal. ·

KATHRYN HARRIS
Taking Chances, Creating Opportunities

by Nancy Rawles

For Kathryn Harris, leadership is constant forward motion. She seizes on change as an opportunity to build on lessons from the past and chart her own course for the future.

Harris, who received the 2008 WIT President's Award, says she was born with a desire to learn and a strong motivation to show her conventional father that men aren't the only ones who can and should be successful professionals. Her determination drives her to keep pushing through to wherever she wants to go. That determination has taken her on a journey from employee to entrepreneur—on a path full of change, challenge, and chances that she turned into opportunities.

Employee to Entrepreneur

Harris always wanted to be a lawyer and was influenced by lawyers she respected to become a litigator. Thirteen years in the field of litigation gave her a chance to work with some great leaders and made her tougher as a professional. But over time, she concluded that it was not the right practice area for her personality. Harris saw herself as more of a collaborator—adept at walking into a situation and helping the business work through it in a productive way.

"Not everything is 'scorched earth and we will battle it out,'" she said. So when Harris had her twin daughters, and found that living with a court schedule and managing twins was a major challenge, she knew it was time to quit her firm. She wanted to see what she could do on her own, build on her own. So she transitioned to in-house attorney, as one of two lawyers responsible for running the U.S. legal and contracts function of a publicly traded Canadian company. She loved the experience of working with business people, human resource professionals, customers, and others. It was this experience as in-house counsel that she would later parlay into the firm she created and manages today, a firm that provides outsourced general counsel services for small to mid-size companies.

Learning to Lead

The road to success wasn't smooth. She founded her firm with a business partner, anticipating that she and the partner were going to build their business together. Then the dot com bubble burst, the going got rough, and the practice needed to be rebuilt. Her partner decided she could not risk slugging it out and grappling with how to rebuild. Harris had to do that on her own. So she worked several years on a reduced income, networked extensively, and provided services gratis to build brand identity, never really knowing if things would pan out.

But Harris has never been someone afraid of change. Not giving up is as important to her as change itself.

Here's what's interesting: Harris did not journey to leadership with the help of mentors who might have taken an interest in her professional development, told her about the business of law, or helped her with her own development. Instead she traveled the "survival of the fittest" road to success.

It was the 1980s. "There were few female partners in law firms, and virtually none in senior management," Harris said. "Executive decision makers and rainmakers were part of the old boys' network."

As a result, women were often left out of the informal social activities where male associates and junior partners connected with "seniors" and got the mentoring or other guidance that helped them advance their careers. It wasn't unusual for female lawyers in the associate ranks to look to the female law partners in their firm for the same type of mentoring and connections.

"Unfortunately, the handful of women who had made it to partner simply did not reach out to young and rising women lawyers," Harris said. "I sense that [they believed] if they had to do it the hard way, then so should those who follow."

That made a huge impression on her and was a definite driver in her personal and professional commitment to mentoring other women, particularly those who are starting out. "The WIT Mentor–Protégé Program was a perfect point of entry into WIT for me," Harris said, "because it allowed me to give the guidance and 'leg up' that women have been lacking in the workplace.

"Every woman of our generation has an obligation to help the younger generation," she added. "I do feel [that in] the last decade [we've] seen a tremendous improvement in the number of women in management and at the executive level and in woman serving as mentors for others. That is a great step forward and something that needs to be nurtured by all of us."

Growing Pains, Growing People

Now that Harris is managing a highly successful practice, she is confronting yet another challenge—learning to rely on her co-counsel to serve the client and deliver the services to her standards. She wants to deliver the best to her clients and knows she can't do it all. She has to rely on her team and trust their work. And when she has to make decisions, sometimes with only eighty percent of the information she needs to feel comfortable doing so, she welcomes the input of others to help her.

Every woman of our generation has an obligation to help the younger generation.

A sense of humor helps a lot. "If you don't have one it's just too darned hard," Harris said. She has always gravitated to people with a sense of humor and looks for that in her staff. If someone on her team is having a meltdown, Harris finds a way to lighten the load, maybe even offering a piece of chocolate.

Being empathetic also helps. "To a point you have to empathize with those with whom you work, your employees, so they know you really care," Harris said. "It takes collaboration, execution, humor, and empathy to be a good leader."

DEDE HASKINS
Busting Myths, Dreaming Big

by Patricia Crew

Dede Haskins, recipient of the 2002 WIT President's Award and the 2006 WIT Founders' Award, is a self-made entrepreneur who has earned respect by taking calculated risks and putting herself "out there." Thanks to her father who served in the Navy, Haskins learned early in life not only to adapt to changes, but also to embrace them. Haskins' hard work and perseverance usually pays off, she says, but it is really her courage to stand up for herself and dream big that makes her successful.

But, like many of us, Haskins wasn't always courageous when she first entered the work force. There was a time when Haskins felt uncomfortable asking for a pay raise. In her first job, Haskins found out that she was paid significantly less than a male coworker for doing the same job. She ended up leaving the job for another, but took a more senior position for the salary she should have been making in the previous position.

Years later, she was promised a pay raise from a departing boss, but after several months, it still hadn't been approved. When she tentatively approached her new boss, he encouraged her to push through the discomfort, saying, "Nobody is ever going to care as much about your compensation as you should, so don't feel uncomfortable asking for what you deserve."

These words changed Haskins forever. "The lesson I learned was that I had to stand up and fight for what I had earned," Haskins says.

"If you don't communicate expectations, nothing will happen," she adds. And, of course, studies show that women typically ask for less and push for less and therefore end up with less—often falling for the myth of needing to pay your dues and have the requisite skills before being considered for a promotion.

But Haskins is not your typical woman, as her career path attests. Today she is the CEO and President of NewVision Health,

Inc., a software start-up that helps healthcare organizations control costs while improving patient care. Though her current business is worlds apart from her first job—software documentation editor for a government contractor—her career moves definitely weren't linear. Haskins believes that serendipity has guided her career path. At every obstacle she faced in her career, she moved left or right as a way to keep moving forward.

"Early on, as an editor, I realized how products are often developed backwards, with the documentation getting done at the end, almost as an afterthought. I realized that I could contribute much earlier by focusing on usability, user interface, and early design activities. By interjecting myself in the process, I learned the 'guts' of how software is developed," Haskin recalls. "I never ran the coolest, sexiest part of the company.... but all my jobs have given me the opportunity to acquire skills, understand the company, meet interesting people, and take on more and more responsibilities."

If you don't communicate expectations, nothing will happen.

Along the way, she ended up leading virtually every function of a professional services or software company, ultimately establishing or running software engineering, customer support, training, quality assurance, professional services, vertical and direct marketing, telesales, human resources, information development, project management, distribution, library services, and creative services departments (in only six companies!).

When Haskins left her last position as a vice-president of marketing and training for a consulting company, she was considering roles as a COO or VP of a division. She met with a friend who advised her to dream big and pursue a CEO position. With no change in her search strategy other than to think of herself as a CEO, a few months later she took over the reins of NewVision Health, where she has been focusing on raising funds and launching a new company with a new product.

KARYN HAYES-RYAN
The Importance of Mentors

by Althea Blackwell

Karyn Hayes-Ryan began working right after college. Since then, she's advanced through the hierarchy of the male-dominated government technology industry. Like many women, she balances daily the demands of family (two children and a supportive spouse) with the demands of the workplace (5,000 employees, 200 programs on the ground and 200 in space) as a Deputy Director in the Engineering Enterprise at the National Geospatial-Intelligence Agency.

One of the keys to her success, she says, is her mentors—the ones she found through professional and personal relationships—and the values with which she grew up and that she incorporated into her life. Here, this recipient of the 2006 WIT Government Award reflects on what she's learned in her journey to leadership.

Bosses, the "Girl Zone," and a Supportive Community

One of Hayes-Ryan's first mentors was her first boss, who happened to be a male, Danny Neal. His encouragement helped her demand respect and display confidence to much older military male coworkers.

Neal provided Hayes-Ryan with the basic fundamentals of the business and became, as she stated, "my guiding light." Not only was he a great mentor, but he also demonstrated to his employees that he was a great father, involved in nurturing and caring for his children. Even after all these years in the business, Hayes-Ryan still maintains her relationship with him.

Another work mentor who helped guide Hayes-Ryan's career and also provided her with a secure feeling was Carol Staubach. Staubach was familiar with Hayes-Ryan's strengths, as she was with all her other employees, pushing them to seek out job opportunities and take risks, but always supplying a safety net to allow them to come back and work for her.

But it wasn't just the work relationships that propelled Hayes-Ryan to achieve her dreams. It was also the personal relationships, including the personal values she observed and used to guide her career. Hayes-Ryan's parents, for example, instilled in her a strong work ethic and a lifelong yearning to learn and grow. Their open communication kept her inspired and motivated.

Another support system Hayes-Ryan holds dear is what she calls "the girl zone," a group of women friends from different educational, ethnic, and work backgrounds. This group meets frequently to network, share ideas, and support one another. The strong bond and close ties among friends help each cope with life events associated with being a professional woman, girlfriend, or mother.

Be honest with yourself and stay true to your goals ... embrace diversity and profit from differences.

Hayes-Ryan believes that the feedback she received along the way was as important as having strong mentors to help steer her career. When she worked in government, for example, she was surrounded with bright and trusting individuals who cared enough to provide feedback. Evaluation from her peers helped her to excel in self-development and prepared her for future opportunities.

Leadership Advice

Hayes-Ryan's advice for aspiring women leaders is to demonstrate integrity—to be honest with yourself and stay true to your goals. Hayes-Ryan also counsels women to embrace diversity and to profit from differences and similarities other employees bring to an organization. She believes cultural diversity in the workplace promotes increased productivity, builds stronger alliances, and enhances teamwork. So she strives to create a workplace environment that encourages learning from others and their diverse perspectives.

Hayes-Ryan says that her own journey to leadership has been an ongoing process of self-discovery and personal growth marked with significant milestones: the collapse of the Berlin Wall and its historic significance and impact on the world; the experience of managing some business programs that succeeded and one that ultimately failed. Even so, she acknowledges, they all contributed to her success.

Holding to her integrity through all of it—the challenges, the successes, the failures—and merging her experience and skills with lessons from her mentors, Hayes-Ryan believes, has helped her become an effective leader. She continues to advance her career by adapting to the changing global and political environment, always addressing greater complexities at multiple levels.

PAULA JAGEMANN
Secretary to CEO — A Cinderella Story

by Martha Padgette

Talk about energy and drive! Paula Jagemann, 2001 WIT Leadership Award honoree, has it. One journalist described Jagemann as a "Type A personality without the bitter aftertaste." The description could not have been more accurate, Jagemann fully admits. "I get pinged for my energy," she says. "I wake up in fast [gear]... [and] I can't slow down ... it is uncomfortable [for me]." But her energy creates a positive surge, rather than a negative drain on those around her.

As the founder and former CEO of eCommerce Industries, Inc. (ECI2), Jagemann knows what it is takes to become a successful entrepreneur. She has seen good times as well as bad. Therefore, she has much sage advice to offer, as well as some great stories of her amazing journey.

The Journey

As a young girl, Jagemann knew what it was like to want for things. She watched how hard it was for her single mother, who often worked two and sometimes three jobs, to make ends meet. Although Jagemann's is a Cinderella story, there was no fairy godmother waving a magic wand. Instead, watching her mother taught Jagemann the value of hard work, and Jagemann reached the pinnacle in her personal and professional successes through earned opportunities, sheer determination, and hard work.

As a young woman, Jagemann dreamed of going to college and earning a degree. Although she was bright and did well in school, it became painfully clear that the funds for this dream were not available. So, she found another path.

Jagemann entered the hotel industry, working long hours at Trump Castle in New Jersey as a reservationist. She later moved to the DC area, married, and eventually became secretary to John Sidgmore, CEO at UUNet Technologies (UUNET) and later WorldCom.

Sidgmore was an intense but well-loved leader, and an excellent mentor to Jagemann. From him she learned that "the right type of leader is one [who] encourages people ... [and has] people [on staff] who complement [the leader's] deficiencies."

While working with Sidgmore at UUNET during negotiations with Microsoft, Jagemann supported Sidgmore in faxing contract revisions between the companies when their partnership deal was being negotiated. Instead of merely acting as fax mistress, she made her own copies of the documents and began making her own mark-ups. Jagemann then compared her markups to those that evolved between the two companies. Her own changes were beginning to match what was being sent back on the "official" documents, and she realized that she was beginning to think more strategically.

When CEO Sidgmore stumbled upon her edits, he sternly questioned why she had not forwarded them. She explained they were her changes and not the official revisions. Sidgmore took a closer look. Sure enough, Jagemann says, "Two of my edits [had potentially huge impacts] to the contract." If she hadn't undertaken this extra activity, she adds, "I never would have learned [the strategy or language]" of these types of deals. Sidgmore then saw Jagemann's true capacity for business and she became an even greater asset to the company.

Later, when UUNET was preparing for its Initial Public Offering (IPO), Jagemann played an important role in pulling the IPO documents together. This included creating the Point-of-Presence map on the back cover of the registration document. Working long hours, she attended meetings not required for her position and learned a tremendous amount about the process. She was ultimately promoted to director of investor relations, and shares that she was "one of only four people on the trading floor ... of Goldman Sachs when the NASDAQ symbol UUNT first went across the ticker. It was as [much of a] goose bump moment as I have ever felt in my life."

Despite her success in business, Jagemann had not given up on her dream of attaining a college degree. In fact, she began attending college at night while working full time and used the IPO experience to write an extensive paper on the subject as a part of her degree in economics. Jagemann was the first in her family to graduate from college. "The degree wasn't for my career," she says. "It was for me—to prove I was worthy."

When UUNET went public, Jagemann became an "instant" millionaire. She, who had struggled to meet basic needs, now had enough money to pay off her mother's mortgage, start college funds for each of her many nieces and nephews, and do just about anything else she chose to pursue. A Cinderella story indeed.

From Cinderella to CEO

Armed with newfound financial security and tremendous confidence, Jagemann did something gutsy. She left her familiar surroundings and launched her own company, ECI2, taking advantage of the networks she'd built during her career. Networks created and maintained, she emphasizes, in a non-self-serving way.

"I haven't always been 'asking,'" Jagemann says. "I have been 'giving' and freely connecting other people with no [obvious] benefit to myself. This way, when you actually do make that phone call, [the person] won't [recoil and] say, 'Well, that's just Paula asking for something.'"

Her philosophy of networking to serve rather than be served paid off when she created her company's board of directors. The names on her list created an instant media buzz. In addition to John Sidgmore, then WorldCom CEO, Jagemann was able to tap Mory Ejabat,

I certainly feel I have earned my place in the world today—it wasn't handed to me. It wasn't easy. It was very, very hard.

founder and CEO of Ascend Communications, and Dan Rosen, direct report to Bill Gates at Microsoft—and all accepted. She says they remembered her "because [I] treated them well [and] got something done for them that was outside my scope... just because it had to get done." She learned that people remember and reward you for those kindnesses. "It is all part of building those networks," she adds, "that I didn't even know or understand the value of at the time."

Jagemann was surprised at the media response to her new board of directors, because she believed the value ECI2 was bringing to the office products market was the real story. But she quickly learned the value of both her networking and this type of press coverage in making her business a success. She went from being a virtual unknown to appearing on CNN and 48 Hours, as well as appearing in articles in Forbes and The Wall Street Journal, among others. This exposure even included a one-on-one worldwide broadcast interview conducted by Bill Gates and his CIO. The visibility was invaluable in launching ECI2 and in establishing its reputation in the office products industry.

Like her transition from poor girl to millionaire, ECI2's success might seem to have come "overnight." However, Jagemann clarifies, her success "... was earned [and not] given to me. I certainly feel I have earned my place in the world today—it wasn't handed to me. It wasn't easy. It was very, very hard."

"I don't know how many secretary to CEOs there are in the world," Jagemann says, "but I'm hoping there are more or [soon] will be." She recognizes she is "... a walking Cinderella story, with a supportive husband and a toddler princess of my own."

The Rest of the Story—and Some Advice

Now retired from ECI2, Jagemann is still running at top speed. She is on the board of a local hospital and is also involved in two different business incubators in her home state of Maryland. After a full life as an entrepreneur, Jagemann likens this tremendous gift of her time, energy, and expertise to a "kind of pay-it-forward ... I am pleased that I can give back some of what I have learned."

So she shares her career experiences with start-up companies and other entrepreneurs. "I don't have all the answers," she readily admits, "but I'll help you find [them]. And that's what I think is more important."

Jagemann again asserts the importance of opening the right doors through networking, including "giving back" through the "connections [that] you can help other people make." And she offers five key points of advice for those in all segments of business or stages of career:

1. Take every opportunity to travel and experience other cultures.
2. Create a diverse network and keep information on your contacts up to date.
3. Give back and help others freely.
4. Extend yourself beyond your specific job title; do things not required—you will learn an enormous amount.
5. Be demanding of yourself, but not so much so that you forget to relish and enjoy your successes more than re-living your mistakes.

Note to aspiring leaders and entrepreneurs: If presented with an opportunity to meet her, grab it!

SUSAN KEEN
Influencing through Results

by Raluca Monet

Susan Keen was taught by her father, an engineer, that she could be whatever she wanted to be. And she believed him.

But Keen, who is now Technical Director of the Navy's largest Business Transformation Program, candidly recognizes her naïveté as a young professional in not fully understanding the career limitations facing women. When Keen started her career in 1978, women were primarily in subordinate positions and only one or two held executive-level rank positions in the Navy. Looking back on her own journey to leadership, Keen notes that the institutional and cultural progress made since then seems like a transition out of the Dark Ages.

Stewarding the Whole

Keen, who received the 2009 WIT Government Award, has a solid academic background in scientific computing and extensive experience in scientific and business information technology programs. Keen's stock-in-trade is to continually reach for emerging technologies to deliver business solutions to her customers. Results matter. In her opinion, everyone has the responsibility to make visible contributions, to chart her own course, and to make choices that break down barriers.

Key to Keen's philosophy is the notion that, no matter where a person sits in an organization, influence can be earned. That person, however, must patiently look for opportunities to contribute and then demonstrate results. As a leader, Keen focuses on creating a vision and achieving results. Her thinking, which revolves around what Keen calls "the art of the possible," inspires her to make a significant difference in the organizational environment around her.

Keen mentors others to create their own value by being a "steward of the whole" rather than an "owner of a part." To find this kind of leader, she advises, watch who people listen to and from whom they take direction. A good leader is steady and provides a compass for achieving designated goals. A leader balances and tunes the workforce, ensuring each person has a valued contribution to make.

"Active engagement by a leader is very visible to the team," says Keen. "People become brave about their own contributions when they feel this stability and the assurance that someone is in charge and aware of the challenges and opportunities the team is facing, and that the course is actively being monitored. This reassurance allows team members to step up to challenges and reach for creative opportunities knowing they are part of something that will be successful."

A Mentor's Example

Be a "steward of the whole," rather than just "an owner of a part."

Keen owes her own success in part to a progression of technology opportunities, and in part to mentors who recognized her talents and energy and who served as examples of how to handle business challenges.

Linda Smith, for example, was one of Keen's early mentors. Smith had originally entered a Command at a low management level and operated in a mostly male leadership group. Keen remembers watching Smith patiently assessing what each man brought to the executive team and then determining what she could bring. She began to upwardly navigate her career by demonstrating her business savvy, and realized that she could bring her superior business experience to the table for the benefit of the team. The results she achieved, combined with her positive attitude and her willingness to be part of the team, earned Smith a place at the executive table.

Based on Smith's example, Keen advises other women to carefully consider when to "play their hand."

Keen's played her hand by using her deep knowledge of technology and her capacity for innovation to help the Navy realize the benefits of information technology. Specifically, Keen has left her mark via the Enterprise Resource Planning program, which means that now a single business system supports the Navy and the entire enterprise, transforming the way the Navy does business and providing financial transparency and total asset visibility.

Advice for the Leaders of Tomorrow

To aspiring women leaders, Keen's advice is to influence through results. She believes that whereas men are often promoted on potential, women are typically promoted on demonstrated results. Obtaining results opens people's minds and causes them to take notice.

Keen also recommends that women help others through mentoring, specifically helping them understand the business, find their place in it, and stay aligned to what is important to the business so that contributions are understood and recognized. She also advises that women support the greater mission of the organization with innovations that improve the organization.

Finally, Keen stresses that leaders should put time into their people, build compatible teams, and support them, saying, "A leader's success depends on the success of the team."

CORINNA LATHAN
Evolving a Leadership Style

by Piper Conrad

"Oh, is that what I am, a leader?" Dr. Corinna Lathan asked herself while attending a Young Global Leader Summit organized by Harvard University. Lathan, who would later win the 2002 WIT Entrepreneur Award, had been selected by the International World Economic Forum to participate in this prestigious summit for young global leaders, but it was not until she sat in class with other young leaders and heard how others defined "leadership" that she began to think about what made her a leader.

And it seemed then that the seeds for leadership—and for the passion she brought to her work—had been planted at the beginning of her career, when Lathan was a graduate student at Massachusetts Institute of Technology (MIT), and rooted in the family values she carried with her as her career, and her leadership style, evolved.

From Research to Entrepreneurship

At MIT, Lathan had taken her lifelong interest in space and decided to research how space affects human performance. This research introduced her to the concept of dual use technology, or applying technologies developed originally for military or related purposes to industrial, commercial, or consumer use. Forging a partnership between Catholic University and the National Rehabilitation Institute, Lathan set up a laboratory to show how robotics could be used in both the medical and defense arenas. One of Lathan's first projects was to develop a glove with pressure sensors that a child with cerebral palsy could use to drive a remote control car and that a soldier with just one hand could use to control a robot.

This project energized Lathan. She saw how research could help disabled children and make a real difference in the lives of the less fortunate. But Lathan knew that she would not be able to take a product to market if she continued to do research. It was that urge to launch products emerging from research and development (R&D) that made her leave academia for a position in a technology incubator, where she became an entrepreneur.

"I had spent my whole life in academics; I did not know a thing about business," Lathan says. "I had experience running a research lab and soliciting grant money, so I took that and parlayed it into running a business and getting funding."

Today Lathan serves as the chairwoman of the board of directors and CEO of AnthroTronix, a ten-person engineering and research company located in downtown Silver Spring, Maryland. Lathan has spun off a division, AT Kids Systems, which manufactures, markets, and distributes products that have emerged from AnthroTronix' R&D efforts.

[Don't just] be something ... do something.

Lessons in Leading Well

"I never said I wanted to become a leader; I never said I am a leader; I just wanted to work on fun projects that help make the world better," Lathan says. "I just happen to have the attributes that people associate with leaders."

Finding herself thrust into the leadership role, then, Lathan looked for guidance on how to lead. From her experience of working under a number of managers, Lathan knew how she did not want to lead. She knew what had not worked to motivate her and her teams. So she stepped back and observed how leaders led their teams. She took notes about everyone—the woman at the coffee shop, her old teammates in sports, her past supervisors. Lathan did not seek to emulate any particular person, but rather to find what was effective in each person's style.

What did she take from all those observations? In a phrase, "pick your battles."

This piece of wisdom was familiar—it had its roots in Lathan's family values, and it gained a new twist when she first started working as an engineer. Her family motto had always been "We may be crazy but we're not stupid." The advice given to her as a woman in engineering was that you had to take on a bull dog mentality and push your way through. Well, that approach never resonated with her. So she creatively morphed that wisdom and refused to fight stupid battles.

That approach served her well—in academia and in business.

"When I was in academia, I could have really fought tooth and nail to get tenure," Lathan says. "But I sat back and thought about what I really wanted to accomplish and [I realized] that academia simply wasn't the answer. What I wanted was to be able to call the shots on what research I did. Tenure was the traditional way to [achieve that goal,] but I decided to venture out and start a company. To me, [starting a company] was a smarter battle to wage than trying to fight for tenure. Ironically, while I was on leave to start my own company, the School of Engineering promoted me and approved my tenure."

The irony prompted a reflection about what she'd heard at the Young Global Leader Summit, where someone defined a leader as someone who connects problems with solutions. "That had always been my definition of an engineer, and I never thought of those two roles being similar," Lathan said, laughing. But given her successful career as an engineer, Lathan could see how she has evolved into a leader.

Defining Success

Lathan's family values not only influenced her leadership style, but also her definition of success. She was taught at a very young age that work was not just a day job; it should be a passion. Proudly reciting a stanza from the Robert Frost poem, "Two Tramps in Mud Time," Lathan calls attention to the line that encourages the reader to "unite avocation and vocation." This feeds Lathan's drive not necessarily to be something but to do something.

"People may call me a leader, but I'm not trying to live up to a label. I am doing exactly what I want to do," she says. "I have the lifestyle I want and am able to influence the things I want to influence in this world. That is my own definition of success."

GINGER EHN LEW
"Accidental" Leadership, Earned Wisdom

by Susan Filocco

Ginger Lew, recipient of the 2001 WIT Leadership Award, is a law school graduate, business advisor to technology companies, General Counsel to the Department of Commerce, law firm partner, Deputy Assistant Secretary of State for East Asia, Deputy Administrator and Chief Operating Officer of the Small Business Administration, founder of the Asian-American Bar Association of Washington DC, Advisor to the Obama Transition team, and now appointed Senior Advisor of the National Economic Council.

On the face of it, this appears to be a well-orchestrated march up the ladder of success. In fact, Lew's journey to accidental leadership is full of unexpected twists and turns. Lew never set out to be a manager or an executive, let alone a leader. However, her lifelong commitment to competence and creativity has made her a natural.

In a frank and informative interview, Lew shared some of her life lessons, core values, and practical advice.

Lost Job, New Opportunities

Lew's business consulting career took its first turn when she was let go by her employer as a result of a corporate merger. Her severance package allowed her to take some time off and be very thoughtful about her next career move.

Born to immigrant Chinese parents who never received formal education beyond the third grade, Lew was brought up believing in hard work. With the drive to do more and to do better, she pitched herself to the State Department, where she began her public policy career.

Lew can now appreciate how much her experience in public policy has helped her in the business world and how her "bottom line perspective" in the private sector has helped her develop better policy in the government arena. A loss of job truly can provide new opportunities, she believes.

Go Outside Your Comfort Zone

While at the State Department (1980–1981) Lew frequently attended embassy dinners without a spouse—causing there to be an uneven number of people at the table. As a result, protocol experts were unsure where to seat her.

To make matters more complicated, Lew's position required her to socialize at gatherings with the other policy makers, all of whom were men. Traditionally the after-dinner protocol required the men to retire to a separate room with their cigars and the women to adjourn to a different room. However, Lew's political responsibilities required her to join the cigar smokers. She realized that she needed to find different ways of communicating without losing a sense of her own identity. So in order to adapt to the male-dominated business and political environment she studied sports—the "Y chromosome factor"—so that she could successfully develop a social rapport with her peers. This was when Lew learned how to go outside her comfort zone and assert herself with confidence.

No doubt that journey impacted what she was later able to do for women, and not just for herself. During the Clinton presidency, for example, Lew was the highest-ranking Asian American appointee in the administration and was invited to be a member of the delegation to the UN conference on women in Beijing. There she was struck by then-First Lady Hillary Clinton's statement that women's rights are human rights.

It was also during that conference, Lew says, that "the light bulb went on" about her reputation. She had traveled late to the conference in Beijing, and when she arrived, members of the U.S. delegation surrounded her saying, "Thank God you are here, many of the Asian countries' delegates had all been asking to meet you." This was the first time she realized that not only was she perceived as a leader, but as an international figure of importance.

She, like many women of her generation, had become a true trail blazer, in a world of few, if any, role models. Harking back to her parents' work ethic, and to compensate for the lack of mentors, Lew decided to over-prepare, to be twice as smart as her competitors. Later, she made a deliberate decision not to have children and not to change her name after getting married.

"I never expected to have it all," she said.

Low-Key Actions, Significant Impact

One of Lew's proudest accomplishments occurred when she worked with Secretary Brown at the Commerce Department. While accompanying the Secretary on a trip to South Africa, her task was to find an initiative that would open doors for black South African lawyers.

At that time, there were two systems of legal practice in South Africa. Black lawyers could learn criminal and domestic law, but they were not permitted to work in any type of commercial practice. Lew decided to include, as part of the U.S. delegation, a group of general counsels from major corporations already doing business in South Africa. Prior to the trip, she spoke to each general counsel individually and obtained an agreement that each counsel would hire black law students as interns in South Africa during the summer.

The announcement of this program gained the attention of the South African legal community and the program continued for several years. "Law schools in South Africa are now completely integrated in fields of study and I would like to think that we contributed to this accomplishment," Lew said. "Low-key actions can have a significant impact; individual actions that support a broader community can have a broader impact."

Low-key actions can have a significant impact; individual actions that support a broader community can have a broader impact.

Advice for the Journey

When it comes to leadership and success, Lew shares the following wisdom:

1. "Network like hell" and learn more social skills. Lew had to work to become more outgoing and sociable. She felt that she needed to go outside her comfort zone of traditional values of internalizing emotions and being quiet in order to be a good leader.

2. Be strategic. Always learn something new each and every day. "The technology business is highly competitive," Lew says. "It's not enough to be smart—you have to be strategic. Know what your goals are and pursue them with passion."

3. Develop entrepreneurial skills early and know how to access capital. To be a successful entrepreneur, you must learn to fol-

low the money. "If there is no money, you will not be able to take bright ideas to the next level," Lew comments.

4. Find a circle of women and form a supportive network. "Organizations like WIT are incredibly important," she says. "WIT provides a personal and professional network in a safe environment." It is important to discuss problems and issues to find best practices.

5. First-time graduate? Get an internship. The practical experience will develop valuable skills and broaden networks. Remember that your résumé needs to be targeted to the person you are trying to reach and focused on the position that you are trying to get. Find out why the position is open and what need or problem the company is trying to solve; package yourself as the asset to fill that spot.

Lew believes that today's environment for women has changed a great deal. Having women in leadership positions has changed the dynamics of decision making. It is now acceptable, for instance, to discuss a broader range of personal and professional issues with colleagues. Lifestyle—i.e., home life and family priorities—is no longer a taboo topic in the workplace. This has greatly changed the office dynamics and has allowed greater balance between work and personal life.

There are more women colleagues with whom to travel the path to success in both private and public sectors—and that makes all the difference in the world.

DEB LOUDON
Keep Revising, Keep Adjusting, Keep Learning

by Cindy Lancaster

Deb Loudon, who in 2003 received the WIT Government Award while she was deputy CIO of the National Reconnaissance Office, is pioneering, bold, and passionate about starting new things. In her career, she's blazed a trail of experiences she called "exciting, invigorating, challenging, and rewarding," and set a standard that many aspire to follow. And, she says, it all began in high school.

Inspiration

Loudon was first inspired to lead when she was captain of her high school basketball team. "When I was young," she says, "I didn't really have [female] role models. [Yet] I knew [women] had so much to offer. I felt that if I did it, if I led the way and showed we could take the risks and accomplish things, we could show results."

This inspiration led to a lifetime of accomplishment. As a young mother in a small Arizona town near an Army post, for example, Loudon saw that there were few activities for young women—so she started a girls' league for eight- and nine-year-olds. She'd had absolutely no experience playing softball, but her team came in third place that first year. Later she was inspired to start the first modeling agency in Arizona. She collaborated with a local community center to teach modeling classes, something she herself had learned after graduating high school. She organized the first fashion shows in the area and initiated mannequin modeling outside the stores in town. One unexpected benefit of these early leadership activities was the rich network she built. "The social aspects," she notes, "were as good as the results of our work."

Her early inspiration continues to influence her vision of the future. "I want our children and grandchildren to have every opportunity that they are willing to work hard to achieve," she says.

Advancement

Not one to be daunted by challenges, Loudon tackled a bachelor's degree when her children were babies, and then two master's degrees when her children were school-aged. She worked long nights and early mornings to complete her course work, while mothering and nurturing her children during the day.

"As a leader and role model for my children," she explains, "I wanted them to learn that education is important, and you are never too old to learn more or do a different job."

But the example and message she sent her children wasn't just about being a lifelong learner. She also delivered the commencement speech. "I gave my undergraduate commencement speech to [more than] 5,000 students," she says. "It was a phenomenal thing for my children to see."

Loudon then entered the workforce through an internship program with the government. Due to her undergraduate GPA, her supervisors allowed her to accelerate through the program, moving up multiple grades every year due to the leadership qualities she exhibited. The program exposed her to information technology and contracting; she quickly realized how much she enjoyed these disciplines.

She had an "aha" moment during the internship—that if you envision a place where you want to take your career, you can create it ... just be ready for it when it comes. And so she defined the type of career she wanted and earned the certifications required to become a CIO. She then tapped into her network to find a way to get there. "I had to market myself and market the job [I wanted] as well," she says.

Failure

Not everything was a smooth ride, however. Sometimes Loudon failed.

"At first," she says, "I thought it was it me. Was it something I was doing wrong?" Loudon eventually realized, as does any good leader, that failure is a learning experience.

"You have to fail to learn and move ahead and get where you want to be," she says. "If something doesn't work—guess what? You just try something else, and try something else, and keep trying, [until you succeed]. Each new thing you do or try gives you one more experience that you can incorporate into your skill set."

Loudon's willingness to try and fail taught her another thing about leadership. "Always stay professional," she says adamantly, "even when things don't go as you want them to. Don't bring yourself down to someone else's level. You need to be and stay a role model and an example. You want people to think, 'I admire you. Will you mentor me?' They have to see something in you that they trust, that they want to emulate."

Lessons

It's one thing to lead, another to understand the power of that leadership and the strength required to sustain it.

"One thing I didn't realize was the impact I would have on other people's lives, how others would feel about the decisions I made," Loudon says. "When I was team captain in high school, I didn't understand the impact of not picking someone to be on the team or of not including someone in a game." Because of this experience she learned how to consider others' reactions to her decisions.

Each new thing you do or try gives you one more experience that you can incorporate into your skill set.

"You lead without even knowing it sometimes," she adds. "You naturally want people to follow your actions and cues."

She learned other lessons about leadership during her career, one being that the farther you go, the more challenging it gets, and the more factors that play into how things turn out. "Success became harder to achieve," she says. "[So] I became tougher as I got higher on the leadership ladder."

One lesson she quickly learned was that hard work alone did not guarantee a step up the ladder. "Nothing could be further from the truth!" she says. "Merit is a big measure of success; not only do you have to work hard, you also have to show value."

You also have to show you can stand your ground, especially if you are the minority in a culture different from yours. "It was more difficult to ensure respect at the table when I was the only woman," she says. But standing her ground, while understanding the culture and respecting differences, eventually earned her the respect of her male peers.

Another valuable lesson Loudon learned was that she must depersonalize situations and focus on outcomes—especially in business. "In a business environment, you have to take the 'person' part out of it and look at larger factors like the competition, environment, culture," she advises. "There are so many external factors [over which] you have no control that play into decisions you make." Loudon now knows to observe these factors and account for them when translating plans into actions.

Advice

"You need to have a plan [when charting your journey to leadership]," Loudon says. "You need to know where you want to go, what you want to do, and how you're going to get there. Bring in people you trust to support you and help you get there; if you don't have [this] support you're not going to achieve."

For this reason, she says, finding a mentor is key.

"Surround yourself with people who encourage you, who help you think through the major decisions of your life," she adds. "Do everything in your plan, [but] make it flexible. Keep revising, keep adjusting, keep learning. Keep taking risks."

Today, as an independent consultant, Loudon embraces the idea that leadership is a journey and thrives in her leadership roles. "Once you become a leader you can't stop," she says. "You must continue on the journey and learn and evolve."

KIMBERLY MCCABE
Lending a Hand to Make the World A Better Place

by Pam Krulitz

Kimberly McCabe received the Women in Technology Entrepreneur Award in 2003 at the young age of thirty-four while CEO of Virginia-based Advanced Performance Consulting Group (APCG). In the six years that followed, she successfully sold her company and joined the U.S. Army staff as a senior executive, where she leads the Army's Enterprise Task Force.

Throughout her life, McCabe has encountered diverse mentors who have helped her with personal and professional growth and validation as she followed her childhood passion: doing her part to make the world a better place.

"Everywhere I've gone, I try to find someone I want to be like, whether it was when I was running my own company, or [working] in large organizations such as EDS or the Army," she says, and focuses on building relationships with people from all walks of life. "For every one person who has tried to [tell me] either explicitly or implicitly that I can't accomplish my goals ... there have been twenty people who have been gracious, generous, helpful, and supportive. I have been fortunate to have many mentors, most of them informal, who have helped me just because they could."

Going First

McCabe's mentors have included Army generals and CEOs, and parents and extended family, even her five-year-old son. "A leader is the one who goes first," her son told her, "and a leader is the one who takes care of all the other kids."

McCabe appreciated the simplicity of her son's wisdom and how clearly it aligned with her own philosophy that leaders "go first" by being courageous, taking responsibility, and establishing a vision. McCabe believes leaders should truly care about the people they work with, garnering loyalty and commitment to achieve a common vision.

Giving Back

A third-generation entrepreneur, McCabe learned about business early in life. As a pre-teen, McCabe began working with many aspects of her fathers' medical facilities. Her duties ranged from helping organize and file medical records to providing administration support and assisting in the urgent care department. Through this opportunity to see a business first-hand, McCabe learned "how businesses ran," adding that she "saw how people in a wide variety of jobs with unique contributions made the business work." And from this, she formed her fundamental belief that a business could be about people coming together to create something beautiful, such as the harmony created by the orchestra McCabe played in as a youth.

I have been fortunate to have many mentors, most of them informal, who have helped me just because they could.

During those early years, she also learned from her parents the importance of embracing ones' fundamental values when building and running a business. McCabe's parents were clear that "it wasn't about making money. It was always about people, values and character," she says. "It was always about giving back and doing the right thing for the right reasons." Those lessons have stayed with her throughout her career.

Creating Community

When, at the age of twenty-nine, McCabe and a partner started their own government consultancy, APCG, it was as much about creating a community as it was about creating a company. From day one, the vision was clear: create an environment where they could follow their own "True North." According to McCabe, "'True North' for us was having a positive work environment, a values-based, high-integrity [atmosphere] and, most importantly, it was a way to have a positive impact on our public sector clients and their organizations."

As McCabe and her partner grew APCG, she reached out to those she respected and found mentors who both challenged and validated her leadership philosophy. From Renny DiPentima, who led SRA International from $300 million in revenue to more than $1 billion, she learned that it was possible for a company to grow and not lose its soul. McCabe says DiPentima "was an executive who ensured that the soul of his company stayed intact—it had to do with the care he had for [his staff]."

McCabe also speaks fondly of another mentor, Dave Humenansky, who is a lead partner at Booz Allen Hamilton. Humenansky has played many roles in her life. They met when she interviewed for a job with him. Although she didn't accept his job offer, choosing instead to start her own company, the interview served as a starting point for a long-lasting relationship. At times they have simply maintained a personal mentoring relationship, and at one point, McCabe's company, APCG, became a small business protégé in Booz Allen's mentor–protégé program.

"He's been a shining star in my life," she says, "by providing counsel, being a sounding board, providing a reality check, sharing thoughts and guidance about how to handle situations, and [giving input on] how to maintain a healthy balance in my life."

And McCabe is effusive in describing the quality of leadership she has experienced during her tenure in the Army. "I am surrounded by brilliant people who are passionate, motivated, helpful, and open," she says. McCabe has found yet another mentor in her current boss, LTG Robert Durbin, about whom she says, "[his] capability and leadership [are] astonishing; he is someone I want to emulate." LTG Durbin has provided her with the opportunity to again live her passion in making a positive and substantive contribution—this time by working in a role to essentially transform the central culture and processes of the Army.

Acknowledging Support, Paying It Forward

As McCabe thinks back on other mentors who have had an impact on her, she sounds a bit like an Academy Award winner who is genuinely grateful to everyone who has taken the time to offer a hand and doesn't want to leave anyone out. For example, McCabe speaks of Ira Goldstein, who would always make time for her, getting together with her every couple of months for lunch and providing sage advice. She then acknowledges Laura Odell, Rob Jones, and so many others.

McCabe now gives back by being a mentor to others and making time to advise other entrepreneurs. For example, McCabe is involved with a non-profit that helps underprivileged women re-enter the workforce.

It is not hard to see that she has taken the wise counsel she has received over the years seriously and has indeed made the world a better place!

DONNA MOREA
Don't Follow a Path—Blaze a Trail

by Kathy Albarado

Admittedly, "leadership" was not a word that occurred to Donna Morea, recipient of the 2002 WIT
Corporate Award, as she embarked upon her career
as a new graduate with a studio arts degree from
Wesleyan University. Her own leadership journey
was one that Morea did not predict or dictate. She
learned early that the mythical career path sought
by graduates was not at all the expected "yellow
brick road" that led to Oz.

Morea has long since realized that the more interesting careers
are the ones that blaze a trail rather than follow a path. In fact, she
muses, the path is really only seen in retrospect—when one turns
around to look back. The path forward is rarely predictable or well-
marked.

This is true of her own journey to leadership, which she describes
as "unexpected." Rather than seek a career in the arts, Morea decided
to combine her creativity with business skills and pursue her entrepreneurial spirit. She went back to school and acquired an MBA
from Wharton School of Business. Joining what was then American
Management Systems (AMS) in 1980 as her first real corporate job,
Morea had no idea that nearly thirty years later she would have led
three mergers at CGI-AMS, and today would be president of U.S.
and India Operations for CGI—a company with more than 25,500
employees in more than one hundred offices worldwide.

Here, Morea discusses the core traits and values she strives to incorporate into her practice of leadership, and offers advice to those
who desire an equally successful career.

Core Leadership Trait: Authenticity

Leaders must be authentic, Morea believes. Authentic leaders,
she maintains, are willing to show their vulnerability. These are

the leaders people want to follow. However, for a leader, there is a fine balance between being transparent and recognizing that your team members will read (or try to read) your expressions, make assumptions regarding inflections in your tones, and analyze your vocabulary and body language. This becomes an issue, for example, when leaders are "tested" by tough and/or uncertain times.

In such circumstances, Morea believes that putting a good face forward in order to instill confidence and maintain professionalism is not necessarily in conflict with the concept of authenticity. According to Morea, people will be inspired and motivated when they know who their leaders are, what they stand for, where they excel, and where their weaknesses lie. She believes strongly that, above all, one should stay true to oneself and to one's core values—hers are communication, commitment, and collaboration—always modeling desired behaviors.

The more interesting careers are the ones that blaze a trail rather than follow a path ... the path is really only seen in retrospect—when one turns around to look back.

Staying True to Core Values

Morea's core values are integral to creating conditions for success: communication, to maintain an open and honest environment where authenticity breeds trust; commitment, which she defines as delivering a great job while fulfilling expectations; and collaboration, because the outcome of a team effort always outperforms that of an individual.

Morea believes strongly in the concept of "team." The best way to build a strong team, she says, is to identify what people do best and place them in roles that allow them to be successful. Successful teams have a shared purpose, understand why they exist, and are clear about their goals. At the same time, their individual members understand how each of their roles fits into the overall team structure. The team then develops a sense of purpose as each individual commits to meeting the goals.

Footsteps to Follow

Like other authentic leaders, Morea is a woman people like to follow. She supports, inspires, challenges, and appreciates her colleagues and team members. Colleagues have shared passionate testimonials of her phenomenal leadership. Having spent time speaking to Morea about her thoughts on leadership, I was not at all surprised why her team would feel that way.

No doubt due to her success, Morea is often asked what advice she would give people as they embark on their career. Her answer is always the same.

"Work hard, find out what you like to do, pay attention to where the company is heading and what's needed to get it there," she says, "and you will find the path, or it will find you."

GLENDA MORGAN
What Luck Favors

by Dianne Black

Zimbabwe native Glenda Morgan began her leadership journey early, though not by intention. While studying political science at the University of Cape Town, South Africa, Morgan happened to learn about the Black Sash organization, a powerful group of women fighting apartheid in the then-segregated country. A passionate supporter of human rights, Morgan joined the Black Sash, becoming a regional co-chair of the organization at the age of twenty-three. There, she says, amazing women gave her tremendous coaching and mentoring, and helped her discover that she was capable of organizing and leading large groups of people. Her experience as co-chair with the Black Sash put in motion a journey that led her to a deeper understanding of the successful qualities of a leader and laid the groundwork for winning the 2009 WIT Rising Star Award as director of technology and learning at George Mason University (Fairfax, Va.).

Morgan developed this deeper understanding about leadership as a result of her foray into a career in information technology. Yes, her undergraduate work had focused on political science. But in the 1990s, Morgan became fascinated by the Internet. She frequently stayed up all night reading about and practicing the latest technologies she was discovering. She decided to forge a career that would combine knowledge from her undergraduate studies with her newly found passion for technology—and so she earned a PhD in political science and successfully defended her dissertation on the topic of technology policy in 2000. Along the way, she made a series of career moves that allowed her to witness leadership close-up—and noticed more bad examples of leadership than good ones. "I learned most from the bad ones!" she says with a smile.

But then she experienced an awakening. While Morgan was Director of Academic Technology Initiatives in the California State University system, a consultant was brought in to assist on a project. At first meeting, she felt they were destined to be completely incompatible. Morgan was, in her words, a "sappy social scientist," and the consultant was "an ex-military engineer." The relationship was "a house on fire," and here again, she thought, was another bad example that she could learn from. To her surprise, the outcome was quite different.

One of the biggest mistakes women can make is not taking the time to network. Networking helps build trust, strengthen relationships, and ultimately achieve one's career goals.

The consultant made Morgan think a lot about leadership. She realized that good leaders are self-reflective and that they excel at listening, admitting that as a leader "I talk a lot... [yet the] people I want to be like as I 'grow up' are good listeners." The consultant provided a great deal of what Morgan calls "accidental" personal coaching. He also bought her Marcus Buckingham's book *Now, Discover Your Strengths*, which she still cherishes. From that book, Morgan learned and continues to practice the simple lesson of playing to your strengths rather than your weaknesses. Her experience with the consultant continues to shape her thinking on leadership to this day.

To wit, Morgan makes it a point to practice active listening, and one would suspect that it has paid off in her networking efforts, another lesson she says learned "accidentally."

"One of the biggest mistakes women make is not taking the time to network," Morgan said. She believes there is nothing more valuable than heading out after work with professional colleagues in a social setting, noting that it helps build trust, strengthen relationships, and ultimately achieve one's career goals. "There is so much power even in weak connections," she says. "[Networking] has gotten me a lot of places [that would not have been possible for me to reach] had I not had the strong network [that] I have."

Reflecting on the many "lucky accidents" that have helped shape her career, Morgan points to several key factors: having early great mentors, working with a consultant who changed her thinking about leadership in a significant way, and learning the power of networking.

Yes, you can call it luck. Or, you can look deeper and recognize the truth of what Louis Pasteur, a "rising star" of the nineteenth century, said about luck, opportunity, and success: "Luck favors the mind that is prepared."

LOUISE M. PEABODY
Don't Overlook Mentors and Sponsors in Disguise

Loyce — Thanks for putting words to my experience. You're the best. Louise

by Loyce Best Pailen

When asked about her own success, Louise M. Peabody, CPA, and recipient of the 2009 Founders' Award, immediately points to those who mentored her, sponsored her, influenced her, and supported her. She is the last to take credit and the first to acknowledge she achieved her success through the generosity of others.

Today, Peabody, a partner at the public accounting firm of Watkins, Meegan, Drury & Company, LLC, exemplifies the "pay it forward" mindset and supports others to repay those who supported her. For example, she is a member of the AICPA and serves on the Ethics Committee of the Virginia Society of Certified Public Accountants. She has also shared her professional accounting expertise—a background that includes traditional audit and accounting services; development of policies, procedures, and internal controls; and Sarbanes-Oxley implementation, cost accounting, and compliance—with Women in Technology (WIT). She previously served as treasurer and guided the organization to financial viability in accordance with recognized standards for nonprofit organizations. She also secured pro bono tax filings for WIT through her employer, and she developed the investment and re-investment guidelines that had been long-standing goals of WIT.

Here, Peabody recalls the professional sponsors and mentors who believed in her, friends and colleagues she trusted for solid feedback, and those closest to her who provided support as she tirelessly sought and achieved her goals.

At Home

Family tops Peabody's list. Who they are and what they achieve profoundly influence her every day. She is quick to express her and her husband Maurie's joy that their youngest daughter just graduated from college. She then smiles wryly and adds that their joy also extends to "making the last tuition payment." Peabody looks much too young to have children in their twenties; yet, she has three. Having raised a family with her husband and achieved professional success at the same time pleases her.

Without hesitation, Peabody thanks her husband for his support and flexibility over the years. Though it was not easy climbing the career ladder while married with three small children, Maurie was always a strong partner and father. Their work schedules always seemed to mesh so they could share family responsibilities. Peabody acknowledges times when her husband had to give seventy percent and she had to give seventy percent, but they succeeded together and always found a balance.

In the Workplace

Peabody's business relationships have provided her with a number of sponsors and mentors—and she acknowledges that most of her sponsors and bosses have been men.

In 1984, for example, Peabody held her first job at a small publishing company and worked for a "visionary" boss who taught at the University of Maryland and held a PhD in information systems and library science.

"He was a different kind of person but understood the value of sharing information," she says. For example, he intuitively recognized the potential value of the Internet. His advanced world view positively impacted Peabody's success in several ways. He encouraged her, challenged her abilities, and introduced her to things that, at that time, went well beyond her sphere of thought and experience. He taught her the value of the printed word and about publishing. He challenged Peabody to stretch and do different things. He charged her to upgrade her writing skills, as well as travel to trade conferences and meet new people.

As with most mentoring relationships, this one had its pluses and minuses. Peabody notes, "There were times when he totally annoyed me and suggested things that I did not want to model." However, he always set high expectations for her, and he always allowed her to achieve that level.

And at Watkins, Meegan, and Drury, where Peabody works today, Mike Meegan and Phil Phillips became her sponsors and helped advance her career. When she joined the firm in 1995, she needed a flexible work schedule to accommodate her family responsibilities. These two men expressed confidence in her abilities. They recognized Peabody's strong work ethic and easy work style—a style Peabody describes as collaborative, which she attributes to being the middle child in a large family—and her ability to work with "difficult people." With Meegan's and Phillips' support, Peabody became the firm's first female partner.

In the World of Women

Getting out of the consulting environment and connecting with other women provides special opportunities for Peabody. She mentions her daughter, Bridget, as someone who is always sympathetic to the stressful situations her mother often faces. Peabody also turns to WIT to find peers willing to give honest feedback and friends to help her move forward.

Peabody specifically credits Fran Craig and Betty Arbuckle with recruiting her into WIT and soliciting her involvement. Peabody took leadership roles on the Nominating Committee and the Women Business Owners SIG and served on the board of directors for both WIT and the Women in Technology Education Foundation. Peabody also volunteered for many years as a mentor in the WIT Mentor–Protégé Program, receiving high praise from those she mentored. Her continued efforts ensure that other WIT members reap the benefits of a vibrant, significant, and substantial organization where they can make meaningful connections, both personally and professionally—just as she has.

As people advance in their careers, they often realize they can attribute their skills to the most unlikely people—people who were mentors in disguise, even though they did not like them.

On Recognizing "Mentoring Moments"

Today, formal mentor programs flourish in many organizations to help young professionals achieve and succeed; however, informal mentoring relationships also play an important role in career success. Peabody finds it interesting, for example, that as people advance in their careers, they often realize they can attribute their skills to the most unlikely people—people who were mentors in disguise, even though they did not like them. At the time, they did not appreciate the teachers who were a little harsh in their grading, supervisors who demanded perfection, and managers who pushed beyond the comfort zone—but these mentors in disguise did influence their overall success.

Having been both a mentor and a protégé, Peabody understands mentoring, and she observes that different people mentor in different ways. We may not like everything about the person who provides advice or the way they deliver it, she suggests, but we always know what a mentor looks like even if we don't recognize it until years later.

Likewise, Peabody believes to succeed, you must develop a special maturity to recognize mentoring moments throughout your career. She counsels that mentors don't always come to you; you must seek them out and ask for help.

"Select people who will take you out of your comfort zone and open you up to new experiences," Peabody advises.

As for herself, Peabody continues to seek opportunities to be with people who are different. She says the knowledge and understanding she gains through those relationships help her appreciate their differences—and relish the experiences they have in common.

LAURIE REYES
Practicing Passion and Perseverance

by Martha J. Padgette

As a child, Officer Laurie Reyes learned about helping others from her father's example. Her father always stopped what he was doing to help anyone who needed it, and when Reyes was with him, she enjoyed the feeling she got from helping others. Further, her father never hesitated to tell his daughter that she could do anything; there were no limitations. These experiences were instrumental in leading Reyes, who later received the 2008 WIT Government Award for her accomplishments, into a career in law enforcement. Today, she is an officer with the Montgomery County Police Department where she has served for twelve years.

When Reyes was approached by her sergeant in 2005 to look into establishing a new program within Montgomery County called Project Lifesaver, she knew it would be unlike anything she had done to date. The program would offer tracking bracelets to residents who had a tendency to wander, such as those with Alzheimer's disease, autism, or Downs syndrome.

Immediately, Reyes discovered a real passion for Project Lifesaver, as she realized its benefits for both the community and other police officers. She knew she could do it; she just had to persevere and overcome any challenges. And there were challenges: public speaking, presentations to senior officers, training and budget drills, and finally selling the program. True to character, she did not let these concerns slow her down.

After some initial work fostering Project Lifesaver, Reyes realized she was indeed "... the right person to sell the program to other officers." It was a hard sell initially, she admits, but her passion for the project drew many to lend a hand. "Soon everyone wanted to help and I wasn't afraid to ask for [or accept] that help," she says.

In retrospect, these weren't the first challenges Reyes had encountered and overcome. At several points in her life Reyes might have given up or changed directions. There were the academic challenges in college. She could have dropped out, but she fought through the frustration and found success. She could have quit the Police Academy, but she drove through the obstacles, gained insight from the experiences, and continued to find success.

In addition to her own perseverance and tenacity, Reyes is quick to point out that there were some very supportive and influential people along her journey who continued to push her forward when her confidence or determination waned or her path seemed unclear. They include her father, her husband, and numerous co-workers and supervisors. They encouraged her not to give up, pointing out the strengths and other valuable qualities that were fundamental to her success. These people were instrumental in helping her stay the course and pursue her passion. Reyes notes that we are often quick to overlook our own strengths and it is a true blessing to have those people in your life, along your path, to help you adjust your perspective.

You don't have to be the star pupil to make a real difference.

Because of her own struggles and the encouragement she received along the way, Reyes is enthusiastic about something else: sharing insights with others, especially young women. She stresses that we each bring more to the table than our intellect or our education. We also likely bring some level of emotional intelligence. According to Reyes, a person with a strong intellect but without emotional intelligence may fall short of success. Reyes suggests that you don't have to be the star pupil to make a real difference. You never know what opportunities might come your way or "what you have inside of you that will make you a leader," she points out, adding that you should accept the challenges and opportunities as they come. And when criticism or feedback is offered, Reyes warns not to take the comments personally. Use that feedback to help you learn from your setbacks and refine your approach. When confronted with a problem, Reyes urges us to "think outside the box of [our] own limitations." If we know our limitations, we can use our strengths to work around them. Although we must be able to laugh at ourselves, Reyes emphasizes that it is vital to avoid self-deprecation. We must be aware of this tendency to self-deprecate, resist it, and allow ourselves to "be humble yet confident." And finally, Reyes reminds us to have passion for what we are doing.

Although Reyes seems hesitant to accept the title of leader in the traditional sense, she agrees that she has been able to lead through her passion. "Leading from the heart has been successful for me," she confirms. "I lead [Project Lifesaver] from the heart and... people pick up on that."

This is acutely evident when Reyes conducts the training for the project. To see a group of twenty officers who are initially hesitant and resistant change by the end of the class is particularly gratifying. Reyes feels successful when she shares with officers something they hadn't yet considered and then again when she sees the benefits the officers gain from that experience.

"I feel the most success when I inspire others to share my passion," she says. Just as she learned as a child, Reyes is teaching and leading by example.

ELIZABETH SHEA
Focused on Building Trusting Relationships

by Piper Conrad

Through a discussion of the challenges she has faced throughout her journey to leadership, Elizabeth Shea consistently weaves a theme of trust and relationship building. Whether it was trust in others, trust in herself, or the building of trust among clients and colleagues, many of the barriers Shea has overcome can be attributed to relationships founded on that elusive quality.

The Entrepreneurial Effort

Shea, recipient of the WIT 2005 Entrepreneur Award, launched herself into entrepreneurship in 1997. She started to build a marketing firm and soon met Kristi Hedges. The two shared a similar vision and decided to create a partnership; the SheaHedges Group was born.

"Taking a partner is hard. You give up some control. It's like entering a marriage," Shea says. "I believed that together [we] could grow faster and more effectively than we would alone. I took a leap of faith that the relationship would work out."

For ten years, the pair grew SheaHedges Group to just under $2 million in revenue and created a brand that was well-known and respected throughout the Washington, DC, technology community. In looking at the next phase of growth, the pair realized they had different personal and professional goals.

"Just as difficult as the decision to take a partner was the decision to dissolve the partnership once it ran its course," Shea says.

The Next Chapter

In 2007, Shea bought out Hedges' share of the business and rebranded the agency as SpeakerBox Communications. Hedges launched her own executive consulting business and continues to share office space at SpeakerBox.

"The transition was very cordial and smooth due to the mutual respect we had for each other's professional and personal strengths and goals. I believed in Kristi and wanted her to succeed and she felt the same," Shea says. "We just realized we would take separate paths. I am happy we have been able to continue working in a different kind of partnership."

The personal aspect of the partnership buy-out proved to be the easiest part. As Shea met with banks to discuss loans and funding she was repeatedly asked, "So you are the sole owner?" She was also frequently asked why her husband did not attend the meetings with her. Banks also asked for a deeper level of financial data than they did of male counterparts who were seeking funding at the same time.

Shea secured funding through a female banker and experienced a record first year.

An Open Book

In leading SpeakerBox, Shea builds relationships through openness and trusts that people will respect that openness. The company financials are shared at bi-weekly staff meetings. Shea explains, "I want [our staff] to feel they have a stake in the company, that it is all of ours to build. You can't help build something when you don't know the status of the financials."

> *I want [our staff] to feel they have a stake in the company, that it is all of ours to build.*

Shea meets frequently with her counterparts at other area agencies and has an open dialogue (as open as is prudent) with them about business and strategy. "Competitors are the ones who talk about you the most in the marketplace," she says. "I want them to be informed of what's really going on."

Trust and relationship building do have a downside, however. "The hardest part of my role is parting ways with an employee or even a client. Being able to step back and say, 'This is not a fit,' is really tough," Shea says. "I find solace in ensuring [that] both parties understand the thinking and are comfortable with the decision."

Shea knows that trust is one aspect of feeling "validated" for who you are and what you have achieved. In that she's no different from the rest of us.

"I am a person who likes validation. As the leader of a company, you don't get a lot of outside validation day to day," she says. "I have used my network of peers outside the company as a sounding board and as a way to fill that need for feedback and, sometimes, a pat on the back."

KATIE SLEEP
Steadfast Belief and Values

by Anne Teehan

Katie Sleep, the founder and CEO of List Inc., recounts that "2000 was the year from hell...what came out of it was an anchoring effect that defined the company." She is referring to a series of experiences that challenged her to focus on what was important in her life and on how she wanted to build and sustain her company, which provides IT professionals to clients that need to augment staff when facing business or technology challenges.

Resiliency

One of the first hurdles that Sleep, recipient of the 2008 WIT Entrepreneur Award, describes is the telecom industry crash—which directly impacted her business' bottom line. Her telecom clients were unable to pay her hundreds of thousands of dollars owed for services rendered. To cover payroll and overhead, Sleep didn't take a salary for more than four years. Sleep remembers that she and her husband "hung on every day" knowing that it was the right thing to do and better days were yet to come. This kind of leadership, one that demonstrates sacrifice and perseverance in the face of adversity, may be a key reason that List Inc. has retained eight of the ten original employees since the company's inception fourteen years ago.

Next, Sleep's personal foundation was shaken when her mother passed away suddenly from breast cancer. Her mother's death caused her to reflect on her own life, the choices she had made, and her values. She'd wanted marriage, children, and a career but found it hard to juggle all three and climb the ranks of Fortune 500 companies. When her mother died, she said she thought she may have "missed the plot" despite her successes.

So, instead of buckling under when the tough times hit, she regrouped, determined to find out who she was, and make the necessary changes. Sleep hired an executive coach who emphasized self-care as a prerequisite for running a company. The result of her coaching sessions was an awareness that now extends to how she's been shaping the company culture and operations. She's intentionally "building the team a different way" and finding success.

Benevolence

Sleep has turned the grief for her mother into a remarkable gift through her work with the Leukemia and Lymphoma Society: she is heavily involved with Team-in-Training. Team-in-Training is the society's charity sports training program for volunteers who want to participate in a sports event (marathoning, triathalons, or biking) to raise money to combat leukemia and lymphoma. Sleep has been involved with a team that undertakes a one-hundred-mile bike ride in honor of someone with cancer, an individual they call their "honored teammate."

Since 2000, Sleep has participated in seventeen of these events. "It's been energizing from a company point of view," she says, and adds that focusing on others through activities like Team-in-Training builds compassion and a "sense of reality and balance [that] has enriched everyone."

What's great about this journey is that I've chosen to be who I am, and it's working.

Work, Life—and Fun

Sleep's son and daughter both work for List Inc. and she is proud of how well they are doing. "It feels good to be in a position to provide management guidance based on hard-earned experience [to my children]," she says.

Non-work family time has increased, too, over the past three years, with regular weekend dinners and fun activities that now include Sleep's grandchild. As a self-described "Type A who is trying to become a B," Sleep says she's proud that she has "done it differently," focusing on her values.

Today, no doubt because Sleep has built her highly successful technology solutions company through leadership based on these beliefs and values, Sleep has a feeling of contentment that strongly contrasts with the upheaval she experienced after her mother's death.

"What's great about this journey is that I've chosen to be who I am," she says, "and it's working."

LINDA KEENE SOLOMON
Sign of a Leader: Helping Others Take Flight

[handwritten inscription]

by Paula Tarnapol Whitacre

Linda Keene Solomon, recipient of WIT's 2004 Corporate Award, is rarely in her office. Her computer sometimes has an in-box full of emails to which she must respond. But to Solomon, a principal with Deloitte, it's more important for her to be out advising her clients and supporting her leadership team and others who are part of Deloitte's Federal Practice. Solomon's focus on her clients and her team's success is revealing of her leadership style. Here, she talks about her own journey to leadership and offers advice for current and aspiring leaders.

Aligning Needs and Opportunities

After helping to establish the Federal Practice in 2003, Solomon is now responsible for Deloitte's account with the U.S. Department of Homeland Security (DHS). "As a leader of a very high-talent team, with close to fifteen partners on the account, what is my role?" she asked. "I need to make my team successful. I have to focus on creating the next set of opportunities for my clients and my team to be successful."

The fact that Deloitte is a partnership, rather than a corporation, affects how Solomon views effective leadership. "In our business, one key measure of success is how many new partners you have 'made,'" Solomon said. "At the end of the day, that means you have created opportunities, you have been financially successful, you've been able to help others develop their talents, and drive overall growth for the organization. Focusing on growing and developing new partners is a really important thing to me."

One way Solomon helps develop new partners is by identifying how to align an individual's talents and passion with client needs and opportunities. "I want to put them in a position to get those opportunities over the goal line so they feel motivated, passionate, and fulfilled," she said. "I need to identify, build, and engage the talent, and distinguish between those who will be part of the next generation of leadership and those who will not. That's a tough subject, but it's very important for leaders to be able to identify top talent."

Although she is surrounded by a steady swirl of appointments and people, Solomon maintains an air of calm. She calls herself an introverted person, but says she extracts herself from a natural tendency toward shyness because of her passion for achieving results, doing the right thing, and helping others succeed. "Those passions have taken me to many places in my life," she said.

Lessons in Leadership

Solomon's first professional experience in a leadership role came as a newly minted Proctor & Gamble project manager in the 1980s. "I was working in all parts of the country—Lima, Ohio; Augusta, Georgia—in manufacturing plants, coming in to work with older white males when I was a twenty-three-year-old young black female," she recalled. "I learned that it's all about achieving results and helping people succeed. If you are sincere and people see there is nothing that will deter you, they come around." Solomon realized she was successful when people who were once wary of her had begun to call her for advice.

I learned that it's all about achieving results and helping people succeed. If you are sincere and people see there is nothing that will deter you, they come around.

In 1990, Solomon joined Deloitte and became a partner in 1997. She moved from Atlanta, where she was supporting global chemical and oil and gas companies, to Washington, DC, to start the Federal Practice. When the DHS opportunity came about, it was important to move quickly to identify members of a team that could deliver results.

"Being a leader meant defining a vision [for] the new Federal Practice and [understanding] this new entity called Homeland Security," Solomon recalled. She also acknowledged the natural hesitation of staff to switch to a new, unproven account, especially for Deloitte employees who would have to relocate to Washington, DC. Solomon emphasized that "in cases like that, leadership is something that you radiate that people can feel. They had to rally around that vision."

Throughout her career, Solomon has played an active role in supporting Deloitte's Women's Initiative, a high-profile, company-wide program that is now recognized as one of the top in the field. In addition to her work with the Women's Initiative and with a host of other company and community activities, Solomon often serves as an informal advisor to women (and men) on the way up. She shares this advice:

- **Carve out time for the people side.** "I tell our women that it goes without saying that you must produce results, but you must also carve out time to establish strong relationships with peers, gain visibility with partners, and develop a portfolio of communications approaches," she said.

- **Add value with your leadership skills.** "It's great to demonstrate good judgment, have strong communications skills, and other internal qualities," she said. "But you have to know how to translate those qualities externally to add value."

- **Be a constant learner.** "Leaders have to be ongoing, constant learners," she said. "Life doesn't stand still. Who would have thought that 9/11 would occur and [the] Department of Homeland of Security would be created? I had to invest in learning about Washington and what the security marketplace was going to look like."

Solomon recounted that her first leadership experience occurred at age five. As a bluebird in the play "Hansel and Gretel," she remembers stepping out of formation to help the other bluebirds learn their moves. The learning is far different now and the challenges are more high stakes, but Solomon still realizes that leaders have to help fellow birds learn to take flight.

LISA THROCKMORTON
Unofficial Mentors, Insightful Guides

by Piper Conrad

"I've had unusually close access to all of the CEOs I've worked with," Lisa Throckmorton commented when we spoke about leadership and mentoring. It is this early and consistent insight into the priorities and challenges of company leadership—through the unofficial mentoring she received from these CEOs—that has helped shape Throckmorton's career.

As an employee of small and mid-sized companies throughout her career, Throckmorton, recipient of the 2002 WIT President's Award, found herself working with people with an entrepreneurial spirit and a "just get it done" attitude. This enabled her to step into roles and responsibilities that were beyond her years or experience and to learn by doing. She is proud that she has jumped on the opportunities afforded by an open, entrepreneurial culture, but is quick to disclose that knowing the business gaps she could fill wasn't always intuitive.

"I am grateful for people along the way who have pushed me to see and take advantage of opportunities that lay in front of me," Throckmorton said. For example, when she was working at SpeakerBox (then SheaHedges Group), two key executives left on maternity leave. Throckmorton, with some coaching from co-founder Elizabeth Shea, took a chance and stepped into the agency's operational and training and development functions. This leap positioned Throckmorton as an agency leader and deepened her experience in the business side of agency life. Her success in filling the gap left by the executives on maternity leave positioned her to create a role for herself within the agency, leading the training and development of account teams as well as overseeing client service.

For Throckmorton, successful mentoring means putting in the time to really develop a relationship. That means engaging in conversations outside her day-to-day job description. The conversations offer insight about the thinking that goes into running a successful company and can reveal hidden opportunities.

"I think building a relationship around a bigger-picture interest in the success of the company allowed my bosses to see how invested I was, how I thought about things," Throckmorton said, "and led them to give me projects that were outside my experience and formative learning opportunities."

Throckmorton has also used networks such as Women in Technology to find mentors. "I served on the board of WIT at a young age (mid-twenties), surrounded by seasoned veterans," she said. "I took the opportunity to just soak in their experience and advice."

It is not what the mentors actually say to you or tell you to do, it is the environment that they provide for you to talk openly and allow you to answer questions for yourself.

Not being intimidated by age or experience is tough, but Throckmorton's comfort in working with CEOs helped her feel at ease on the WIT board. That comfort and confidence opened her up to conversations that helped shape her view of available professional opportunities.

"I had a great respect for the women on the board and was happy to earn their respect as well," she said. "I found if you work hard and pull your weight, people quickly overlook your age."

Throckmorton's one formal mentor was Clyde Northrop, an advisor to SpeakerBox Communications. Throckmorton refers to Clyde as her "work therapist" and used their monthly meetings to talk through challenges and opportunities. He knew her strengths and provided skillful guidance to help her discover the best path forward.

While professional mentors often encouraged Throckmorton to plunge into uncharted territory, her drive for success can be traced back to her mother. Throckmorton's mother worked throughout her childhood and inspired her daughter's own ambitions. "Starting with answering phones at the church rectory," she said, "I could see that I was completely in control of my earning potential and job path."

Throckmorton has learned that the best relationships take an investment of time to cultivate. In the end, it is not what the mentors actually say to you or tell you to do, it is the environment that they provide for you to talk openly and allow you to answer questions for yourself.

Chapter 3
Advice

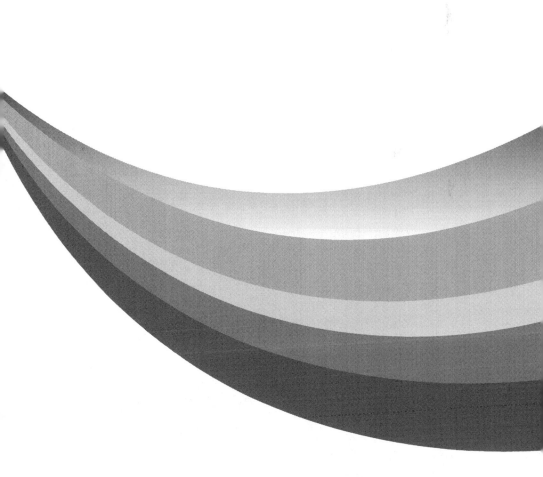

BARBARA ANDERSON
Focus on Goals, Stay Connected

by Marnie Bloom

"Make a decision and move on" is Barbara Anderson's motto. "Inaction is worse than a wrong decision. You need to keep moving."

And so she has done. Throughout her career, when Anderson, who received the 2006 WIT Corporate Award, saw a job that needed to be done she took it on. She would start by consistently establishing a visionary, big-picture perspective, and then translate that vision into executable items. Results and reaching a goal motivate her—and there is always a plan to achieve those results and reach that goal. Throughout her career, Anderson has used this vision-and-goals approach to motivate her teams. She's learned a lot about what makes a team successful, and shares that here, along with some advice for the next generation of women leaders.

Connection Is Key

In addition to the focus on goals, Anderson says, the key is to stay connected to a distributed workforce. Anderson, for example, is currently with EDS, an HP company, as the vice-president of its Global Healthcare Industry Group, with responsibility for all U.S. state and local government healthcare business. She manages a geographically dispersed team of almost 5,000 people. However, during her first ten years in the workforce, Anderson worked in an office environment with her teams.

"It's one thing to manage a team when you can look them in the eye," she says. "It's another thing when you see them maybe twice a year."

During the past fifteen years or so, Anderson has managed her team remotely. She believes the key is to make time to stay connected. This could be as simple as taking five or ten minutes between meetings to make a quick phone call and stay in touch with staff. She takes advantage of tools and technology to ensure that everyone is focused on the same goals. In addition to staying connected, technological advancements have enabled Anderson to maintain a reasonable work-life balance, since she can communicate with her team from her home and during off-hours.

Light Touches Make a Big Difference

Despite her emphasis on keeping in touch, Anderson would not describe herself as "touchy feely." Yet, she says, it is the "light touches" that can make a big difference. Her various mentors over the years have encouraged her to provide more of these touches to her team, and she has found that this approach is resoundingly worthwhile.

You can do anything you want to do. Identify what it is and do it!

Even though Anderson herself does not need a lot of feedback, she does realize that constant feedback may be a critical need for those around her, that others may not be motivated in the same way she is motivated. And in motivating a team, the best approach may even be to go against your own grain. A case in point: Her team was at a training program held at a Disney resort. The program happened to coincide with an important sale closing. The other leaders convinced her to come to the program wearing Mickey Mouse ears to celebrate the win. Although it definitely wasn't her style, it was a huge hit with the team. People are still talking about it even after ten years! Doing it for the team made the difference, she suspects, because as she discovered, success is about the team, not about the individual. It is the team that will get you there, she says.

Goals Are Golden

"Young girls do not have limits!" is Anderson's leadership advice for the next generation. "You can do anything you want to do. Identify what it is and do it! You do not need to know exactly what it is right now. You can change your mind. The main point is to have the goal in mind; keep working toward it."

MIRIAM BROWNING
Chance. Confidence. Courage.

by Cathy Hubbs

Forty years ago, Miriam Browning applied for an administrative position with the Army in Berlin, Germany. Able to type only thirty words per minute, she thought her chance of getting the job was slim. Instead, she was called in for an interview and then hired. "You have a college degree," they told her. "You are intelligent, and we can get you a security clearance."

Browning seized that opportunity. Her ambition, candor, and confident intelligence catapulted her into a distinguished thirty-five-year career with the Department of the Army. During her career she observed, participated, learned, and led as she rose to the position of Army Deputy Chief Information Officer, a federal Senior Executive Service position—and later won the 2002 WIT Government Award.

After retiring from the government, Browning became a principal at Booz Allen Hamilton where she further honed her leadership and technology expertise. Currently, she is president of her own company, where she partners with industry clients to provide strategy and business development services to small and large businesses seeking contracts with the federal government. With her rich history and experience, Browning offers the following salient counsel for aspiring women leaders:

- **Lead with integrity.** Your words and deeds comprise your reputation throughout your career, so make sure you are honest and ethical in dealing with people and in making decisions.
- **Cultivate ambition, i.e., the passion to excel.** Set goals and seek champions. Set aggressive promotion goals and align with senior leaders to serve as your mentors and advocates. Those leaders will then champion your rise in the organization. In Browning's experience, when a man is promoted to a new position, he immediately asks what he needs to do to get promoted to the next

position. When a woman is promoted to a new position, she immediately asks how she can succeed in the new position. The lesson? Always focus on your next career aspiration.

- **Maintain balance.** Keep a consistent temperament in all situations and treat individuals equally and fairly. Balance work and life commitments for your own sanity and for a richer career. "I know a very senior woman executive who was chastised by higher management for being too '24/7,'" Browning says. "She consistently sent emails at 2:00 A.M. and expected her staff to respond quickly. It's one thing to work long hours for a special or surge project, but to do so constantly sends the wrong messages and often results in less effective decisions."

[Self-promotion] is a learned art, and I think women should seek out mentors (men or women) throughout their careers who do this well and continuously learn from them.

- **Set a vision, and think strategically.** "I can think of many times in my career when I just wanted to do something grander and did so," Browning recalls. As an example, ten years ago Browning created a single career field in the Army for all IT professionals with a goal to improve education and advancement for more than 20,000 people. To successfully execute that new initiative, Browning had to envision an end-state, get stakeholder buy-in (the hardest aspect), change existing policies and procedures, put a management process in place to accommodate the end state, and then measure results.

- **Exercise seasoned judgment.** "Seasoned judgment is a critical characteristic of a great leader," Browning believes. "After discussions and the voicing of many opinions, someone has to filter, synthesize, and move ahead with a decision. A leader must have the self-confidence, mental acuity, and experience to do this." She finds that many people, on the contrary, prefer others to make the decision. The result could be shortchanging their own growth. "Decision making and seasoned judgment improve with use and experience," she says, "so learn these capabilities early and practice often!"

- **Deal well with people.** Last, but not least, a successful leader must have the ability to deal well with people. "Interpersonal relations are often the discriminating factor in terms of who gets ahead in an organization," Browning says. "More likely than not, the congenial 'people person' will be selected for promotion over a more technically competent but interpersonally challenged person."

Leadership Lessons

Browning attributes much of her success and wisdom to the "senior executives who believed in me and my abilities—the ability to set a vision, work well with people, and make tough decisions."

She admits, though, that she'd like to have known some things when she first began her career—things like self-promotion. "This is a learned art," Browning says, "and I think women should seek out mentors (men or women) throughout their careers who do this well and continuously learn from them."

Browning also notes that not all leadership lessons are obvious. Here's her take on three specific lessons she learned through experience:

1. **Don't treat men as equals.** Though conventional wisdom says treat everyone alike, Browning offers a different perspective. "Men and women are different. Each processes information, communicates, and makes decisions differently in the workplace," she says. "Appreciate the differences and leverage them appropriately. For example, women excel at team building and collaboration; men excel in highly competitive environments. Assess the situation and blend the best of both."

2. **Go with your gut.** "In the past, women had to be extraordinarily fact-centric and highly technically competent to succeed," Browning explained. "However, the intuitive aspects of today's work environment require different skills for success. Collaboration, peer-to-peer networking, Web 2.0 capabilities, and team building require abilities such as sharing ideas and tasks, consensus building, and working in a non-command-and -control environment. The 'lone ranger'—male or female—is no longer an aspirational success model."

3. **Get a mentor.** "A mentor or a peer confidant is essential to learning [the rules of the success game]," Browning says. "Often, men are more naturally mentored, e.g., through golf, bars, sports events." Contrasting that natural mentoring with her own experience, she notes, "Women must seek mentors as they rise in an organization. Leadership can be lonely, and a mentor can help. Learn to be both a mentor and a protégé as you go through life."

KELLY HARMAN
*She Not Only Plays by the Rules—
She Makes Them*

by Paula Tarnapol Whitacre

Kelly Harman, CEO of Zephyr Strategy, Inc., and recipient of the 2009 WIT Entrepreneur Award, turned frustration with an employee into a leadership credo that provides advice based on lessons learned, sets expectations for herself and others, and expands on concepts she found most important in developing her own leadership style.

The Twelve Rules

"About ten years ago, [an employee in a leadership role] came in to tell me she couldn't meet a deadline, but it wasn't her fault because a person who reported to her had slipped up," Harman recalled. "That really frustrated me because if you're in charge of a project, everything is your responsibility."

That night, Harman began to think about what she had learned from fifteen years of working with both good and bad bosses. In an hour, she composed what she now calls "The Twelve Rules of Success." Harman has since spent many hours refining them, but they remain her touchstone. These rules are required reading for job applicants and members of her teams. Through word of mouth and media coverage, they have traveled throughout the United States to Canada and Europe.

So what are Harman's "Twelve Rules of Success"? Posted in full at www.the12rules.com, they challenge individuals to think independently and creatively, chart what they want from life, and actively pursue their goals. Harman's earlier frustration with her employee became Rule #11: Take responsibility when it isn't your fault.

Harman provided other examples of her rules. There is Rule #1: Disagree with me. "My employees need to feel comfortable questioning me," she said, adding that "they may see things that I have not seen." Or Rule #4: Tell me you want my job. "I was able to go to my bosses and tell them that I aspire[d] to be a CEO," Harman said.

"They helped me learn ... [they] guided and mentored me." However, she noted that not all workplaces (or bosses) accommodate the kind of directness she advocates. "Sometimes you have to temper [these] rules with self-preservation, especially when you have an insecure boss," she admitted.

If you think what you are doing here is just a job, then quit. Come in on Monday and start your career.

The Entrepreneur

Zephyr Strategy is Harman's opportunity to put her rules into practice. The firm provides strategic marketing services, helping clients (predominantly tech companies) capture new customers, retain existing clients, and grow revenues profitably. Harman launched Zephyr Strategy in 2003 after many years in tech sales and marketing management positions. As Harman recalls, "I turned forty, and I realized it was now or never [to start my own company]."

But Harman didn't merely emerge as the successful CEO of her own company overnight. She began her move toward becoming an entrepreneur early in her career while dealing with the challenges of being a young single parent. At age eighteen she became a mother and the primary provider for her son. "At that point in my life," Harman noted, "my main goal was to have a comma in my checkbook on a regular basis." In those days, she usually held more than one job, juggling her responsibilities as a parent with the demands of multiple bosses. She started several small ventures, including a children's outerwear company and a calligraphy service.

Some of her single-parent struggles eased in 1990 when Harman married. She now has two stepsons in their late twenties and her own son, now twenty-eight. She is also a very proud grandmother. Yet Harman considers those early years of struggle critical to her development as an entrepreneur and a leader.

Lessons Learned

Harman believes the decisions she makes now as an entrepreneur carry higher risk, from a financial standpoint, than those she made while employed by others—even at a senior level.

"As an entrepreneur, each decision I make has a huge impact on my team," she said. "Fifty thousand dollars can be the difference between a line item in a big corporation and bankruptcy for a small firm."

One of the decisions Harman made early on stems from her own experience juggling multiple jobs and worrying how to balance work and caring for her son. Zephyr Strategy employees now work from their own homes with regular communication via phone, instant messaging, web conferencing, and periodic face-to-face meetings.

Although she launched her company from the basement of her home, Harman moved to a large, well-decorated set of office suites a few years later. She quickly realized this move was more a monument to her ego than anything else since these offices usually sat empty. (That expensive office rental may apply to Rule #7: Make bad decisions, since the important corollary to the rule is to learn from one's mistakes.) Now, a small office in a Manassas industrial park provides physical space for brainstorming sessions.

So, in addition to giving her staff—currently all women—the flexibility they need to pursue work-life balance, her updated business model's lower overhead and ability to expand and contract more easily benefits her bottom line. Moreover, the flexible environment helps to cultivate the teams' complementary skills.

"We may be doing a conference call at 6:30 A.M. before the kids get up or at 9 P.M. after they are tucked into bed," Harman said "but we produce." And they heed rule #12: Quit your job. She explains this rule: "If you think what you are doing here is just a job, then quit. Come in on Monday and start your career."

Teenage mother, multiple job-holder, senior manager, entrepreneur, and aspiring public speaker and writer—Harman's own path is testament to her twelve simple but powerful rules. And these rules—Harman's credo—provide perspective and insight for those aspiring to lead or looking to define a new approach to their careers.

MARGUERETE LUTER
On Doing the "Impossible"

by Madelyn Clark-Robinson

From an early age, Luter knew that the difference between what would be possible and what
would be impossible in her life lay in her ability
to imagine herself doing the impossible and the
determination to get the impossible done. These
two qualities—insight and grit—have taken Luter,
recipient of the 2008 WIT Founders' Award and the
2003 WIT Champion Award, into senior leadership
positions in two multi-national corporations and now into the role
of president and CEO of her own consulting firm, The Process Pro.

That journey and its challenges have taught her not only what
makes a good leader, but also how much all leaders owe to their
supporters. Here, she shares some of the struggles, successes, and
lessons learned.

No One Succeeds Alone

Though some leaders come to the role "by accident," Luter made
an early and conscious choice to lead. Her mother, who often
stepped into leadership roles in her community and workplace, was
one of her first role models.

Other role models followed as Luter began building her career,
first at Xerox Corporation, and then at Unisys. She owes much, she
says, to those who lent their support and provided guidance.

"Champions, mentors, sponsors, I had them all, and I have been
each one to a wide variety of people," she says. "I had people who
invested in me, encouraged me to stretch and grow, enabled me to
learn through new assignments, and who were willing and able to
give me feedback that made a difference."

Luter realized the value of having champions and sponsors early
in her career, when both she and her current boss were competing
for the same assignment. A colleague who was part of another work
group overheard Luter's boss denigrating Luter after a meeting, and

approached Luter to get his own, unfiltered take on the situation.

"He closed the door and asked me to talk about how I thought I was doing," Luter recalls. When the colleague heard Luter's version of her current work performance, and after reviewing the documentation that supported her performance, he took it upon himself to set the story straight with the senior leaders.

"From that point forward," Luter states, "he truly was a sponsor—he [spoke] up for me." By the end of that year, Luter had secured the critical assignment she wanted. To this day, Luter remarks on how this colleague decided on his own to support her—she hadn't solicited his sponsorship. "Not only that," she says. "He put his personal capital at stake when he didn't have to."

Focus less on yourself as an individual and more on what you can do to help the people around you achieve success.

That experience, among others, taught Luter that she, like all good leaders, owes her success to others. "No one gets to success or to an executive position by [herself]," she says. "And because of the help they received, [good leaders] step up and offer to fill those roles for others."

The Courage to Grow from Challenges

Early in her corporate career Luter learned how important it is for leaders to exhibit the courage to go where they need to go, even if they are feeling uncomfortable because they are swimming against the crowd or are perceived as different from the dominant culture.

Luter, for example, faced what she says was the toughest challenge of her career when she was one of only two African-American females progressing within the information technology (IT) services industry. Two key situations, however, allowed her to flourish in the face of roadblocks and dead-ends that threatened to slow down or altogether halt advancement in her career.

First, Luter built a network of people inside and outside the companies at which she worked. Those networks included colleagues, friends, and family—people she could trust to keep her best interests in mind. The support, mentoring, and coaching she received enabled her to stay focused on her goals, deal with roadblocks, and remind herself how competent and determined she was.

Second, Luter recognized kismet when she saw it: She was in the proverbial right place at the right time. The right place was Xerox Corporation, the right time the 1980s when the company was executing its commitment to expand the definition of leadership to include minorities and women. Xerox was reviewing and revising its practices, policies, and processes to ensure that all women and men of color would be prepared for and also presented as candidates for positions of power. This, combined with structural changes (for example, employee affinity networks actively sponsored and supported by senior executives) that had begun a decade earlier set the stage for getting women and men of color the visibility, support, and sponsorship that had not been available to them previously.

And this was where Luter succeeded in doing what had been formerly impossible—to thrive, as a person of color, in the corporate environment. She seized the opportunity to demonstrate and be recognized for her leadership competencies: getting people committed to the same vision and working toward shared objectives, thereby freeing the team's "collective genius," and providing the clarity that led to developing business processes that served the organization's mission and goals.

"People need to know where we are going together and why, what it will look like when we get there, and what contribution each individual can make to the team's success," Luter says.

As a result of her efforts, Luter was selected for a senior-level promotion and became a successful and recognized leader at Xerox, and later at Unisys.

Integrity, Authenticity—and Advice

Collaboration and courage aside, a leader must also have core values that guide her leadership actions. For Luter, integrity and authenticity come to the forefront.

"Doing what I say I will do is always most important to me. I want people to know that they can trust me to get things done," Luter says. "But even more important, when I look into a mirror I want to make sure the person looking back is someone I respect and admire. When I complete a job, I want to know I have done [well] and ... made a positive difference."

Her advice for aspiring leaders?

- Focus on growing yourself, making yourself competent in your area, and interacting with others.
- Be committed to continuing to learn.

- Think in terms of contributing to operational excellence and finding more effective ways of organizing and leading people and work.
- Focus less on yourself as an individual and more on what you can do to help the people around you achieve success.
- Understand what needs to be done and find ways to help.
- Make a difference.
- Bring all of yourself, authentically and enthusiastically, to the work you choose.

DEIRDRE MURRAY
Know When to Make the Next Move

by Rebecca Mann

The career path of Deirdre Murray, the 2008 Lifetime Achievement Award and 2001 WIT Founders' Award winner, reads like a page of present-day telecom history: she's had stints at GTE, USWest, Sprint, and now Qwest. Murray credits her success in this rough-and-tumble market to being swift, smart, and savvy about knowing when to make the next move.

When Sprint hired a new CEO and announced the company would move out of the area, for example, Murray's professional instincts impelled her to do her homework and leave the company quickly. "Wait and see" was not an option. As a result of her swift action, she landed her present position at Qwest.

Decisions like this weren't always so easy to make. In the early days, she received little career guidance. Instead, she relied heavily on friendships—particularly with other women—and on her networks for coaching, mentoring, and advice. Then she connected with the team that founded Women in Technology (WIT).

"When we started in the mid-1990s, there was a real thirst for an educational and networking association focused on the interests and advancement of professional women in the field," Murray said. She believes her active engagement over the years with WIT positively influenced her career by keeping her connected to and positioned in her chosen market.

Being savvy about those markets was, and still is, a key factor influencing Murray's success. For example, though she began her career on the commercial side of the telecom business, she soon learned that government agencies spend $70 billion annually on telecommunications products and services. Consequently she redirected her career into government sales.

Murray also attributes her success to keeping her market knowledge up to date. She stays in touch regularly with people in and around the telecom industry. She also finds the media particularly important. She carefully follows press coverage of her customers, and she gets to know the journalists who write about them. Through these connections she develops market intelligence, which helps her recognize opportunities and make smart business and career moves. Likewise, Murray recognizes the impact of technology and stays a step ahead of her clients. She follows the social media and observes their influence on her customers.

Outside her work, Murray mentors young people. Her advice to them is simple. She encourages them to be voracious readers. Reading inspires and motivates. When she meets with clients she always notices the publications on their coffee table—then reads what they read. It provides that all-important market knowledge and helps Murray connect with her customers. She

Be nimble, be smart, and keep a close eye on the market.

also encourages her protégés to be ready to make their next move, advising them to prepare constantly for new opportunities by assessing their strengths and interests, and—here it is again—their knowledge of the market.

Murray's success bears witness to her own advice, "Know when to make the right move. Be nimble, be smart, and keep a close eye on the market."

JENNY MURRILL
Take Advantage of the Domino Effect

by Page Bostic

Sharing advice about networking is common among leaders, mentors, and protégés. But when Jenny Murrill gives advice about networking, she isn't referring to the hasty exchange of business cards that characterizes some networking events.

Instead, building relationships with those you lead is the first commandment of networking (and leadership). Murrill, who received the 2007 WIT Rising Star Award, says, "It's easy to build a network, but the key is to maintain it. This requires significant effort, but can pay significant dividends."

The relationships Murrill built over the years have created one opportunity after another. "Success in your career can be a domino effect," she says. Her award nomination, in fact, was submitted by a colleague with whom she'd worked years earlier. Soon after receiving the award, the dominos started to fall, touching off new opportunities. Murrill received other industry awards, speaking engagements, and executive mentor invitations to senior executive leadership meetings. The domino effect was "spring-boarding" her career to the success she has created today.

How do you build the kind of relationships that will create this kind of domino effect? "You take the time to relate to people personally," Murrill says. "As a leader, you give your team ownership in projects, which heightens their energy and loyalty."

One might speculate that she learned this lesson during her formative years. As a child, Murrill loved math and science. It came naturally: Her father, a computer science professor, was her first mentor. Developing math and science papers during her growing-up years was the norm.

Today, Murrill serves as a role model and mentor for the communities in which she lives and works. With bachelor's and master's degrees in systems engineering from the University of Virginia, Murrill has committed herself to the engineering profession and is a cost and risk analyst for Northrop Grumman's Information Systems sector. She applies statistical methods to predict the cost of complex systems development, production, and operations/support for intelligence community customers. As a Northrop Grumman section manager, she is responsible for the professional development, performance evaluation, and general welfare of her employees. She is also involved with business development and project staffing within her department. Murrill's independent cost estimates often become part of the Congressional budget, and she provides analysis that influences decision makers at the highest levels of the intelligence community.

Create boundaries so that you can achieve a balance between work and life.

She describes herself as a steady leader, one who likes to keep an even keel, taking in everything that's going on around her. She is all about planning, time management, and delegation.

"[Leadership] is a balancing act," Murrill says. "A lot of people want your ear, expect you to make decisions quickly, and expect those decisions to make everyone happy. You have to manage others' expectations and know when to take the reins and when to empower other people to act." She, like many women leaders, wears different hats to enable her to be the leader that she is.

But empowerment isn't just about delegation and inspiration. Murrill adds excitement and passion to the mix. If others are excited, she believes, it inspires them to create an environment that makes the job easier all-around.

She also believes in investing in the people who are interested in the work at hand, and suggests that whether you are starting your career or just a new position, "be positive and show initiative"—in other words, go beyond what's expected.

"Give 110 percent in everything that you do," she says, "but look at the big picture to determine how perfect you need to be and balance delivering a ninety-nine-percent solution versus a ninety-percent solution."

Murrill also suggests creating boundaries so that you can achieve a balance between work and life. As leaders, we must be the one to set the boundaries, she notes, saying "it's important to have an outlet ... to know what you need personally to cope with challenges that arise in both your professional and personal life." Murrill herself is an avid runner. Running allows her to clear her mind.

There is a lot to learn from being involved in "extracurricular activities," too, she believes. Her running during high school taught her "grit and determination." Being on the forensics team gave her the foundation for her technical speaking career in engineering; it prepared her for keynote speeches, panel discussions, college recruiting programs, and her regular briefings with high-ranking government officials.

What does Murrill say to women in technology who are self-conscious about being a woman in a male-dominated field?

"Show that you have confidence and competence and they will see through your age and gender," she says. "Focus on your job. Put your head down and do a good job and you will build respect as a result."

ELLEN QUINN
Live Your Dream

by Anne Teehan

Do you remember the 1988 movie Working Girl? Ellen Quinn does. In fact, she's lived her own version of it.

In the film, Melanie Griffith's character, Tess McGill, has earned her degree while working full time as a secretary. Tess is smart, ambitious, and eager to put her knowledge to good use. She's had one hard knock after another when she finally finds a boss who gives her a chance. Tess's boss, Katharine Parker (Sigourney Weaver), is an executive with a Wall Street investment firm. She came from "old money" with all the wealth, connections, and trappings that entails. Katharine encourages Tess to share her ideas and promises to help her advance. Tess is thrilled until she learns that she's been double-crossed and Katharine is taking credit for her work.

Like Tess, Quinn spent ten years working her way through college. In 1988, she finished her undergraduate degree then began graduate school. Meanwhile, she was in a junior position as a marketing and communications specialist for a satellite communications company with aspirations for more. Her boss, "Sally," was the marketing director.

Sally, like Katharine, came from a wealthy family and had a strong sense of entitlement. Sally viewed people from backgrounds different from hers as "beneath" her, as "servants to be stepped on." (Fortunately, Quinn was unaware of Sally's limiting beliefs.)

Quinn, ever the go-getter, talked to "lots of people" including the chair of a brand new Quality Council who invited her to attend an upcoming meeting. She could barely contain her excitement; she had found an opportunity to shine! Shortly before the big meeting, Quinn ran into Sally in the hallway. The conversation came around to the council meeting and Sally pounced on it, saying, "You're not being paid to attend meetings. You tell me what you were going to say to the chair and I'll go."

This early encounter had a lasting impact. Rather than falling victim to bitterness, Quinn used this experience and others like it to shape her character, her leadership style, and her career. Quinn has pursued a path of personal excellence, using her time and talents to provide opportunities for other women to learn and succeed. Her awards for this work include receiving the Women in Technology (WIT) Volunteer of the Year Award in 2006, 2007, and 2008, and the WIT Champion Award in 2004.

According to Barbara Lee Strosnider, one of the award nominators, Quinn "is the ultimate role model for anyone (male or female) in the business world. She does what needs to be done and does not stand around waiting for someone to give her recognition."

Etiquette is a make-it-or-break-it factor. Do a good job, tell others what you're doing, and pay your dues.

Today, Quinn leads Quality Programs Management for Northrop Grumman and is also a Six Sigma Blackbelt with a wealth of experience working with teams to evaluate and improve repeatable processes. She has convinced Northrop Grumman senior management to be a WIT sponsor in the past, raised funds for the March of Dimes, chaired committees, and continues to contribute to several WIT programs and events.

If that's not enough to leave you breathless, consider that Quinn has been a valued member of the Technology Council of Maryland for fifteen years and is currently instrumental in developing women leaders through the Women in Northrop Grumman (WiNGs) program at Northrop Grumman.

Her experiences "toughened her skin" a bit and lend credibility to the words of wisdom she now offers others. For Quinn, etiquette is a make-it-or-break-it factor. Saying "thank you" and treating others with respect are essential. Though Sally discouraged her, she didn't kill Quinn's dreams of being in the quality field. And she encourages others not to give up.

"That's not a Hallmark card phrase," Quinn says. "It's true."

She admits it's not easy; the real world can be tough and people can have hidden agendas. "Do a good job, tell others what you're doing, and pay your dues," she says.

Clearly, that's paid off for her. Tess would be proud.

DEBBIE THACKER
Commit to a Vision of Excellence

by Page Bostic

The most important leadership trait to Deborah "Debbie" Thacker, recipient of the 2004 WIT President's Award, is enthusiasm. Thacker, former principal, Thacker Associates, who is now with Unisys Federal Systems as Senior Manager of Real Estate, believes in the importance of leaders being excited about their business.

"A job is not a job—it's a part of your life because it's a reflection of who you are," she says.

To Thacker, enthusiasm is giving the best you can even for tasks you do not want to do. "Enthusiasm means you look forward to work each day and influence the success of a business," she adds. "It's a commitment to a vision of excellence."

Thacker believes that enthusiasm can buy time for skills that a leader does not have but needs to develop, and always brings positive energy to a team. "Attitude is often contagious and integrity is the value on top," Thacker says.

Backstory

When she began her career working for a small real estate company, Thacker had had a variety of experiences. The most memorable was in the 1990s when Thacker leased 116 rooftops in downtown Manhattan and, within a fifteen-month period, started her own company providing telecom services. Thacker expressed (with enthusiasm!) how fun the adventure was, all as a single mom with three boys in tow.

Soon after her success, the telecom world and regulations changed, and Thacker's career path also changed. Through it all, however, she built a reputation for a collaborative leadership style, according to colleagues Bill Baker, COO of BTL Services Inc., Sterling, Virginia, and Dede Haskins (see p. 48), who were interviewed about Thacker in a 2004 article for the Women in Technology newsletter, WIT.Word. According to Haskins, "[Thacker] does a nice job of laying out objectives and building a team [that can deliver]. She gives people freedom to execute their objectives, and follows up in a supportive way so that she's not micromanaging."

Reflections—and Advice

Thacker believes that the career one has chosen, or in some cases stumbled upon, reflects the person's traits, education, strength, and personality—and how that leader works is a reflection of personality, ethics, and standards.

Even when it doesn't feel like success, you are still moving forward.

When Thacker reflects on how she got to where she is today, she realizes that she did not focus solely on her career and her position on the so-called career ladder. Instead, she paid attention to what other leaders did, embraced the styles that fit her well, and learned lessons from some whose styles she did not particularly admire. Thacker credits WIT and other professional organizations for making a difference in her understanding of how people function in business. Not surprisingly, then, Thacker encourages young women to step outside their offices and get involved in organizations outside their employer's.

"If you don't find a mentor," she says, "find a group of people who know you and understand you professionally."

To get known in an industry, Thacker encourages writing about topics for which you have expertise. In 2003, for example, she wrote two articles about her work in the industry that became feature articles in two major publications. The value of this experience, as she sees it, is not only the sharing of knowledge among leaders, but the exposure she received with each publication. The articles had an impact on her business, lent her credibility with clients, and are still recognized and leveraged today.

Women leaders should trust their instincts and have the confidence that comes only by having experiences and—on occasion—failing in those experiences. "Even when it doesn't feel like success, you are still moving forward," Thacker states.

And she again comes back to the qualities that she believes have most enhanced her own leadership style—"Persistence! The ridiculous level of enthusiasm."

Quite simply, Thacker notes, it's not much fun without it. Enthusiasm makes a job easier; it makes life easier. And it's something that's within our power to achieve.

"How we spend our day and behave," she says, "is a choice we all have."

SALLY TURNER
Networking Is Paramount

by Cathy Hubbs

"Get out ... and do some networking," says Sally Turner, winner of the 2003 WIT President's Award. "Get to know ... your competitors, people in your industry, people outside your department!"

Turner, who is now the director of strategic initiatives at CGI Federal in Fairfax, Virginia, is justifiably emphatic when speaking of the importance of networking to one's effectiveness; it was a lesson she had to learn herself. In her first career immersion at Wang Laboratories, for example, the culture at that time did not promote networking. Moving to another position with a different company, where the culture was different, taught her networking's value. Upon reflection, Turner realized that the insular contact she experienced in that first position was detrimental not just to her career, but also to the company as a whole.

"We talked almost exclusively with each other—before, during, and after work hours," she says. As a result, communication became limited to internal discussions, making change difficult (if not impossible) and unwittingly stifling creativity. Turner remarked that this strategy would quickly sink a company trying to make it in a competitive global market.

Nevertheless, Turner cautions that we not ignore the importance of networking inside one's own company. Join cross-functional groups, she recommends. Eat lunch with people in other departments. Familiarize yourself with the company's mission and strategic goals. "[Otherwise], if you get promoted," she explains, "you are like a fish out of water: not understanding what the larger organizational goals are, or should be."

Turner notes that networking has other benefits, too. "Networking helps you make friends," she says. "You begin to know people everywhere. Resources abound for fielding questions, finding people to fill staffing gaps, or even provide opportunities should you find yourself in need of a new position."

Some of the impetus for Turner's career success might have come from what she experienced in the small town where she grew up. Turner remembers having a strong desire to get out of that small town and experience the world. Most girls she knew were going to be nurses or get married. In contrast, she says, "I wanted to be a math major and eat spinach."

Don't say you will do something without following through—this will damage your reputation in the industry.

When Turner first got into the computer field she had no idea what she was going to make of her career. She just knew she "would make it work." She noticed men winning awards, and declared, "I am going to win an award." And that she has! Besides winning the WIT award, she's also garnered recognition from groups such as the Industry Advisory Council and companies such as CGI, Wang, and Digital. She then quietly adds that she now has several boxes of awards from years of career and volunteer contributions.

Volunteering, she notes, is another great way to expand your network and broaden your experiences. "Volunteering requires active participation, taking on responsibilities, and becoming actively engaged. Membership alone won't do it," she emphasizes. "Get on a committee; roll up your sleeves and do some work. Don't say you will do something without following through—this will be damaging to your reputation in the industry."

When asked for her thoughts on leadership, Turner underscores that a collaborative approach is imperative, particularly when working outside your field of expertise. Listen, gather opinions, and encourage others to contribute, she advises. Leadership does not always require consensus building and agreement; often it is about providing a safe environment and promoting the sharing of ideas.

As for career advancement and personal growth, Turner stresses that we challenge ourselves. "Leave your company at the top of your game," she says. "If you don't, you will get complacent, lose your edge, and [miss] opportunities."

This wisdom is striking—because, frankly, it is hard to know when you are at the top of your game. However, Turner asserts that it would be a mistake if she didn't encourage us to program ourselves to be vigilant in self-awareness, to recognize the signs of having reached a peak or a plateau at a company. Again, networking can help here: Use your connections as a litmus test in determining whether it is time to move on.

Turner again emphasizes that networking is paramount to being successful. "Fortunately, I am an extrovert, making it natural for me to want to get out and connect," she says. "If you told me I had to stay in my office, I would probably get squirrely."

So Turner is always on the go, "making it a point to make connections and build communities of practice." As a final coda, she advises aspiring leaders to recognize that success comes from being resourceful—and that expanding your world of connections provides you with a lifeline whenever you need one.

MARY WALL
Be the Main Event

by Kathy Furlong

Mary Wall, winner of the 2003 WIT Founders' Award, has advice regarding strategies for job focus and career growth for those at all levels within a company.

She starts by asking a simple question: "What are your duties?" It seems as easy and straightforward as a job description. But understanding which duties and decisions are part of your job, and the roles and decision levels of each person with whom you interact, enables you to get the big picture of your organization. Once you know the world in which you are navigating, you can make conscious decisions about carrying out the high-value duties you were hired to perform.

Wall believes that it is important at some point in your career to have worked all stages of your department's function end-to-end to understand all aspects of the well-oiled machine. Regardless of where you end up, Wall asserts that you will be better skilled overall. Additionally, the more proficiency you have, the more "they" need you. That said, Wall strongly urges that we be careful not to overextend into the roles of others, or take on more than is appropriate for our position.

During the process of understanding your duties, as well as the duties of those around you, Wall notes that you also need to learn what is not part of your job so that you do not dilute your talent. For example, if you perform your old duties and your new duties, Wall warns that you may be focused in the wrong areas. If you don't identify clearly where your responsibilities start and end, you may even cause organizational stress by creating role confusion.

Wall encourages aspiring leaders to allow their support departments to do their jobs, too—so that they do not perform duties for which they are not being paid or take on responsibilities for a title that they cannot put on their résumés. Besides, doing so would mean they are doing the work without the authority or the compensation.

"Think back to the point [where] your job duties changed," Wall advises. "Were you aware that this [change] was happening? Were you directed to take on more responsibility or decision-making authority? When did you start being the 'happy helper' [instead of] requesting the bigger title and pay?"

Though you still need to know how to do each job in case you have to stand in for another employee, Wall emphasizes that you need to recognize when to build a strong team rather than perform each task yourself, insisting that you must clearly understand when to "manage" versus "do" the work and learn to get results by managing others. It can be inefficient and perhaps de-motivating to a team when a manager is trying to do the work rather than guide the team through the larger project.

Learn about the money—that is how you stay in the room as the deal develops and eventually closes.

Although Wall acknowledges that having a good client relationship is important, she warns that relationships alone don't pay the rent. You also need to close new business. Early in your career, she suggests you learn how much time, and under what circumstances, your company wants you to work directly with your customers.

To be considered a highly valued asset by your company, Wall believes, you must know your expertise inside and out as well as understand the financial components that make the business tick. "Learn about the money," Wall urges, "especially if you don't want to—that is how you stay in the room as the deal develops and eventually closes. She who understands the financial side of a bid has the power."

Wall notes that this is a skill few people have, which makes it all the more powerful.

"You may have to work harder to get close to the numbers," she acknowledges, "but you will not be viewed as a serious player [until] you understand [them]. This is often the [key] area withheld from people the longest."

In other words, don't be just a door opener; be the main event.

Chapter 4
Legacies

KATHY ALBARADO
Setting a High Bar

by Pam Krulitz

An early mentor taught Kathy Albarado that success would come from freeing herself of self-imposed limitations. It's a theme that appears again and again in Albarado's own career, and in the values she tries to pass on to her employees and to her children.

Early in her career, the CEO for whom Albarado worked gave her large responsibilities that were clearly out of her area of expertise. After having spent a few years in a variety of human resources positions, Albarado found herself in charge of a shipping department and later running a technology project. She managed to deliver on those responsibilities and learned firsthand what it felt like to stretch herself to achieve more than she thought she could. Now, this recipient of the 2006 WIT President's Award is stretching herself as an entrepreneur, growing a vibrant HR consulting firm serving technology companies.

Albarado's passion for challenging herself and others to set the bar high seems to seep out of the vibrant orange walls of her office. It permeates all that she does. Her voice fills with excitement as she describes a challenge to her staff: "September? I bet we can launch the Apollo awards program by June! How can we make that happen?" Likewise, she expresses exasperation with others who don't seem to share her enthusiasm for doing hard things well.

Not only does Albarado challenge her team at every turn to do their absolute best; she also has a sharp eye for ability and talent that may not appear on a résumé but that is lurking within her employees. She has confidence in them that they may not always have in themselves:

- They haven't ever negotiated a contract with a client? No problem. She believes they're up for the task. In fact, she believes it so deeply that they begin to believe it in themselves.

- No college degree? No problem. She encourages them to roll up their sleeves and learn what they need to learn, with the support of helpful colleagues and access to training.
- If a consultant thinks her own expertise is limited and a client needs someone with more experience? No problem. She provides less confident consultants resources and support, which allow them to exceed expectations—their own.

As one employee told Albarado, "I know that if you give me an assignment, you believe I can do it. I just need to have confidence in myself that I can do it."

Albarado's commitment to helping others be their best is at the heart of her parenting philosophy as well. When her children come home from school or sports with disappointing results, they now know the first question she'll ask—did they do their best? The conversation doesn't center around whether the grade is "good enough" or better than their classmates', but rather on whether there was any way to eke out a little more effort, or put a little more into it to achieve more than they thought they could.

Just doing something is better than sitting around talking about it. You can always adjust along the way if you start getting off track.

Clearly, part of Albarado's secret to freeing people from their own self-imposed limitations has been in setting a high bar. Many other leaders do that, too, but find only frustration as people feel discouraged about or incapable of reaching high expectations.

Albarado's formula for getting employees to meet her high expectations has a few more ingredients: her deep understanding and acknowledgment of how much of a stretch she is asking of people. She knows she's taking them out of their comfort zone by pushing hard and she doesn't do it blindly. She acknowledges the risk. But she is committed to building an organization where ordinary people can do extraordinary things.

"Just doing something is better than sitting around talking about it," Albarado says. "You can always adjust along the way if you start getting off track. That in and of itself is a form of feedback."

In this way, she provides equal doses of support, encouragement, and confidence to go along with the challenge. And that is a formula she'd like to be known for in years to come.

JANICE CUNY
Galvanizing a Community, Nurturing Seeds of Inspiration

by Cathy Hubbs

A large picture window directly behind Janice Cuny's desk floods the room with natural light. Cuny, winner of the WIT 2007 Government Award, has graced the windowsill with a beautiful orchid reaching toward that light, and her walls with pictures of family and of dramatic snow-capped mountains, each scene featuring a river persistently wending its way through the landscape. Taken together, it all seems like a metaphor for Cuny's life as scientist, academic, volunteer, mother, and advocate for computer education and for foster children. And in talking with her, it becomes clear that Cuny's background—as suggested and represented by these artifacts—is rich with experience, interwoven with incredible opportunities and hard work, and infused with a strong passion for improving opportunities in the field of computing for students, as well as for women, the disabled, and under-represented minorities. It is this legacy that she hopes to leave, through her exceptional work and enthusiasm.

Pioneering

As one of the first one hundred women admitted to Princeton, Cuny recognizes she was given an opportunity that women before her had not received. After completing her doctorate, she was awarded the IBM faculty development award. This award was created to provide women in the field of computer science an opportunity to break through the proverbial glass ceiling to become full professors.

After she received the IBM award, Cuny was invited to attend the Computer Research Association's Committee on the Status of Women in Computing Research (CRA-W). Here, she found herself surrounded by powerful, action-oriented, proactive women. The

CRA-W's primary goal—to attract women to computer science and engineering research and education at all levels—inspired Cuny to spend the next thirteen years actively working with that group to provide opportunities for young women.

Galvanizing

In 2004, Cuny was presented with yet another incredible opportunity. She was invited by the National Science Foundation to spearhead a program to increase opportunities for women, under-represented minorities, and people with disabilities. Working for the NSF, she launched the Broadening Participation in Computing (BPC) program.

"Since 2000, high school students' interest in the field of computer science and information technology has dropped by nearly seventy percent," Cuny says. "Currently only one percent of incoming college freshmen are interested in computer science."

Students often do not get a good understanding of computing in high school because they may not have an opportunity to study it, she explained. In many high schools, computing may be offered as a vocational course, not on the track taken by college-bound students. Often these courses teach just basic computer literacy and students may not see the power of computers in problem solving or the range of related applications. They may overlook the societal impact that a career in computing could achieve.

Students often do not get a good understanding of computing. They may overlook the societal impact that a career in computing could achieve.

The BPC program aims to change this scenario by encouraging more students—especially those who are under-represented, such as women, persons with disabilities, and other minorities—to pursue studies in the computing disciplines. How? By galvanizing a national community around these issues. This community of 200 strong recently met to discuss best practices and ways to scale their efforts for larger impacts.

"[This is the] cool part of the job," she says, "working with committed people." She hopes, through the BPC, to provide the resources to amplify their reach.

The BPC program is also working to improve high school computing for all students, Cuny adds. Her current goal is to get 10,000 teachers in 10,000 schools prepared to teach a new, three-course curriculum. She also wants to provide opportunities for ongoing professional development. The hope is to produce graduates who are savvy enough to know when and how to leverage technology as part of a solution: people who are not just users, but creators, of technology.

Nurturing

It is not surprising, given Cuny's life experiences, that she has dedicated her career to providing opportunities for our country's under-represented populations. Cuny and her husband, for instance, adopted three children from the foster care system. This became the catalyst for her to serve as a Court-Appointed Special Advocate (CASA) for other children in foster care, which she has done for the past nine years. She finds the work so meaningful that even in retirement she'd like to work full time for CASA, "helping to ensure that children don't get lost in the legal system and are placed in a safe, permanent home."

Her commitment to the under-represented shines as brightly, strikes one as profoundly, as that collection of light-infused artifacts that populate the office from which she works. The mountains suggest the heights to which she is willing to climb, and the powerful rivers, her tenacity and passion for moving the BPC program toward its goals. And like the orchid reaching for the sun, Cuny continues to reach out to others, creating and perpetuating a legacy of a life imbued with meaning—and light.

ANGELA DRUMMOND
Not Taking "No" for an Answer

by Kathy Furlong

Watching her father run a successful business from home, Angela Drummond had a front-row seat to witnessing the rewards of owning one's own business. It's where she learned the values and traits that would shape her own career, the most prominent of which include a strong determination and vibrant passion. This background and these qualities would help guide Drummond on a journey to establishing her own legacy, a journey that included establishing her own company and the honor of receiving the 2005 WIT Founders' Award.

Very early in her career, Drummond realized she wanted to help facilitate efficient and effective collaboration across the federal government. She was absolutely certain the need for this skill set existed. Drummond did the market research and talked to others in the market space to get their perspectives. Armed with information and confident that she was onto something big, Drummond presented her pitch regarding this potential opportunity to her boss. Much to her chagrin, her boss held an opposing opinion: that it was not such a great idea.

Disappointed, but even more determined, Drummond continued her research and expanded her networking. She truly believed that she had something the industry needed and was not going to give up on her idea.

Then she got her break. One of the people with whom Drummond had been talking had a client who was interested in pursuing Drummond's idea.

Though still in the very early stages of her career, Drummond took a leap of faith and quit her job. SiloSmashers was born.

Although Drummond was full of passion and potential, she had had very little experience running a company. She also lacked female role models in key leadership positions or who had a background in business ownership. Therefore, she had to cultivate her own insight into the qualities of and approaches to leadership that would ensure her success.

"I believe that everyone should develop [his or her] own pillars to live by and stick to them," Drummond says. "These are mine and they [have] really helped me maintain the determination to keep going in [both] good times and bad."

- **Perseverance.** Decide what you will not compromise on to be true to yourself
- **Passion.** Believe in your dreams. Others will see your enthusiasm and will want to follow you and help you achieve those dreams.
- **Surround yourself with quality people.** Align yourself with advisors who share your values and who are smart. The wisdom you get will make you a better leader to your employees.

Her strategies for launching Silo Smashers suggest a fourth pillar: thinking long-term. Drummond knew that she would be competing with larger, better-known companies. So she focused on branding her company so that it would present a clear identity in the marketplace.

I believe that everyone should develop [her] own pillars to live by and stick to them.

"From the very beginning, I concentrated on what we were going to be known for in the industry," Drummond stated, "and decided that [determining] what work we would not do would be just as important as what work we would do."

What does SiloSmashers do? Well, true to Drummond's passion, she made it her business focus to provide "collaborative management consulting services" to the government as well as private sectors. This included offering program management and change management support services to her customers.

Her timing couldn't have been better. Government was shifting towards "downsizing, right-sizing, restructuring, and process improvement." The challenges associated with these culture and business shifts were something SiloSmashers was founded to help support. "Effective collaboration within and between organizations," she explains, "breaks down the silos that stand in the way [of the ultimate goal]."

As a small start-up company in a large competitive market, the need for name recognition was vital. And, of course, this was the inspiration behind the choice of the company's name. "I knew that people might not know exactly what [SiloSmashers] means, but they would remember [the name]," Drummond says.

Staying true to her dreams and passion to provide collaborative solutions to her broad spectrum of customers became her ultimate recipe for success.

And that is the legacy that Drummond would like to leave: to be known as a thoughtful leader who made a significant impact on the efficiency and effectiveness of collaboration across the federal government.

ARDELL FLEESON
Her Office? The World

by Nancy Rawles

Ardell Fleeson, 2007 WIT Champion and Associate at CB Richard Ellis in Tysons Corner, Virginia, chose to be interviewed during a breakfast meeting at the McLean Family Restaurant, a neighborhood diner that has been around for years. Driving to the location, I regretted not meeting in her office so I could get a good sense of her in her surroundings. I arrived first, settled into a booth, and brought out my laptop.

But once Fleeson came in through the door, I understood why she chose to meet me at the restaurant. She waved to me across the room, stopped by quickly to introduce herself, then excused herself to say hello to a few people. Off she went, stopping at several tables, greeting people with a bright smile and clear blue eyes that look right into yours as she speaks.

Eventually we settled in; the waiter stopped by our table and knowingly filled her cup with decaf coffee. Throughout our conversation, people stopped by our booth to say hello and she always introduced me into the mix. I got the message pretty easily: The world is Fleeson's office. I should not have been surprised; her bio states that she lectures regularly on "How to Work a Crowd," serves as a deacon at Columbia Baptist Church, has provided sales training for high-tech start ups, was Membership Director at the Tower Club during the height of the dot com boom, and has been dubbed Virginia's Queen of Schmooze by *Virginia Business Magazine.*

Fleeson seems a force of nature, an energy that will live on through the connections she gets such a charge out of making. An accomplished business woman, singer, public speaker, and deacon, Fleeson doesn't envision a tangible legacy, something concrete you can touch and feel like a plaque or charitable foundation (although she would like to start a foundation if she had the money). If she were writing her own obituary, it would say no one loved people like Fleeson, no one connected people like Fleeson; she was a force for good in the northern Virginia community.

The Personal Touch

Doing good may be a function of Fleeson's faith. Faith motivates her; doing God's will in her life is the energy that runs through her head and into her fingers, channeling energy and faith outward.

Fleeson has great compassion for people who are out of work and facilitates three support groups for job seekers: one for Women in Technology, one through her church, and a new one specifically for chief financial officers. She gets inspiration from her daily spiritual reading, removes the more religious references, and uses the readings to encourage the job seekers.

At the same time, each job search is personal. People open up to Fleeson and she is adept at honing in on their individual situations to provide the right support. Her gift is her ability to connect with people and to teach others how to make connections that will move their careers and professional lives forward. She recalls helping people with difficult life transitions and goes on to tell the story of a gentleman from a different culture who made an appointment with her to talk about his job search. He had spent twenty-two months blindly sending out résumés. He had a PhD, was extremely bright—and was clearly a man in trouble professionally and emotionally. She told him that people in this country don't get jobs through websites and advised he get a job to sustain him while he looked for work. Fleeson told him to work at Nordstrom as a shoe salesman.

The notion of life balance is false. But if you pursue your passion, then [everything] will all fall into place.

Many men have egos too big for that, but not this gentleman. He went to work at Nordstrom, lost thirty-five pounds, and learned a lot about American business. After two years, he stabilized and was able to resume his original profession at the National Institutes of Health. This is the kind of impact of which she is most proud.

Find Your Passion

Earlier in her career, Fleeson's ambitions and career goals were different from what they are today. Although her career will never be complete—the "R" word, "retirement," is not in her vocabulary—she now just wants to make the money she needs to have a nice life, travel a lot, help more people, and be near her children in their adult lives. Her career is not a means to an end; it is her means to a good life.

So what is her advice for girls and younger women? It's an unusual take.

"When I hear that more girls should get involved in math and science, and that women should make up fifty percent of the board room, I hear kind of a sexist view," she says. "Women are smarter than men and better parallel processers. Find your passion and run with your passion. If technology is your passion, then pursue it like any other passion. The notion of life balance is false. It will never be achieved in northern Virginia, it's just too hard-charging. But if you pursue your passion, then [everything] will all fall into place."

At the end of our conversation Fleeson, ever the supreme networker and connector, picked up the tab and gave me the names of two references and two sample readings. And when I got back to my office, she had already emailed me with two referrals.

TONI TOWNES-WHITLEY
Phoenix, Rising

by Pam Krulitz

Toni Townes-Whitley, recipient of the 2006 WIT President's Award, is serving as the 2009–2010 president of Women in Technology. She is also VP and Managing Partner, North America, at Unisys Global Industries.

During her life and career, she's faced some challenging circumstances. "I've been through some really tough times in my life. My kids call it the crumbs in the cereal box, when there's no flakes left—just dust," she says. "I've been there—I've been down to that dust."

Townes-Whitley says that getting down to that point, "to the bottom of your self," as she puts it, makes you ask certain questions. Like "Why not?" Why not take risks you might not have considered before? Why not try something complex, strategic, unconventional?

"So you come back, I'd like to say, like a phoenix," she says, explaining that she had strong family support that encouraged her to "think out of the box," and a strong belief system. "You just rise up because there's no other direction to go. And you don't care so much about whether it sounds all that acceptable or beautiful, you just lay it out there."

Townes-Whitley doesn't dwell on the challenging circumstances she's faced in the past. Instead, she looks forward, seeming to have risen up from the dust with a clear view of what's important for leadership, the legacy that she'd like to leave for Women in Technology, and the courage to pursue it.

Townes-Whitley describes herself as a "balanced leader"—someone who can consistently put together a team and a strategy that will sustainably produce results over time. Indeed, in high school she was voted "Most Likely to Succeed" and "Best All-Around." She is most proud of the All-Around Award. It reflects what is most important to her—the ability to think systemically, and to bring together diversity of thought for the good of the whole.

Once, for example, she led a team that represented seventeen different nationalities. They exemplified her definition of success—the break-through performance a team can achieve together by providing balance (through complementary and contrasting capabilities) to each other.

Her focus on balance applies to professional skills as well. Townes-Whitley appreciates colleagues who have a clear expertise in their profession, or a "major," and who also have a "minor"—something they're also good at that complements their main area of expertise. Townes-Whitley took this view even in her approach to making the most of her college education. In her sophomore year at Princeton, for example, she applied to the Woodrow Wilson School for Public and International Affairs graduate program, which would offer her more interdisciplinary study. Although economics was her major, she reveled in the opportunity to study other fields like public policy and understand the relationships among them.

Her view of the skills needed to be successful in the twenty-first century reflects her emphasis on systemic thinking and balance. In her generation, she remembers, "We had very few inputs. There were three TV channels and two radio stations. There was very little information coming in, and from that, we had to create something."

Contrast that with today, where so many media and internet channels regularly drench us with information. "The challenge now is to streamline, funnel, filter, and frame the message," Townes-Whitley says. "It's a different set of processes from creating, exploding, and expanding [a message]." These processes require taking many bits of disparate data and making sense of it—it's a nonlinear synthesis rather a linear analysis.

In fact, she applies this kind of nonlinear thinking to re-frame the old question about work–life balance. In the generation when she came of age, the message women heard was that they could have it all—a job and a family.

"You can have it all," Townes-Whitley responds, "but not at the same time. There are trade-offs and timing that have to be considered. It's about integration... about accepting nonlinear paths in thinking and in our careers."

Which she herself did—taking seven years off from the tradition-al workforce to be a stay-at-home mother, and finding that it was the most reflective time in her life. She concluded that she had to spend a significant quantity of time with her young children to determine what "quality" time meant for each of them.

"I wasn't just at home with my kids 'eating bon-bons,'" she says. "I was indoctrinating my children by establishing, teaching, and modeling the core values of our family." While she was at home, she also connected with and encouraged other mothers. Through her work on the "Mothers At Home" Board of Directors, for instance, she was able to support at-home moms through her articles in *Parenting* magazine and other publications, and through radio appearances and Congressional advocacy for the Homemakers IRA.

[Today] it's about integration... about accepting non-linear paths in thinking and in our careers.

And today, Townes-Whitley is bringing her leadership and her skill at systemic thinking to Women in Technology as its president. The legacy she'd like to leave to the organization is to bring it balanced performance. She'd like to ask the questions that will ensure the organization's relevance in a world with more "inputs," when it's important to have both a major and a minor in one's expertise; when careers take nonlinear paths; when global teams are becoming more the norm; when the use of technology is integral to many jobs but is the main focus of fewer; and when there are many more types of technology (for example, nanotechnology, biotechnology, and green technologies) making an impact on the world.

Townes-Whitley is bringing together many diverse voices to respond to these issues and answer the questions they raise. And she will wade through the myriad inputs and opinions. She'll work with her team to find the common thread among the disparate programs to get to the essence of what the real purpose of WIT is for the next generation. And, success will be the team's—not just hers alone.

Risen from the dust? Indeed she has—balanced scorecard well in hand.

Appendix A

Women in Technology: Contributing to the Success of Professional Women in the Technology Community

Women in Technology (WIT) was founded in 1994 to offer women in the technology community in the Washington DC region an environment for networking and professional growth, so that they could extend their relationships and create new business opportunities. WIT is a not-for-profit organization dedicated to creating a forum where women in technology can be recognized and promoted as role models.

Now nearly 1,000 members strong, WIT provides programs designed to help expand women's networks, grow their businesses, or find their next career opportunity. These programs include

- monthly meetings on a variety of topics with a diverse array of speakers;
- special interest groups (SIGs) to address audience-specific issues such as diversity outreach, executive women, women business owners, technology, and sales and marketing;
- member networking luncheons at various locations in the DC Metro region;
- Girls in Technology (GIT), which provides support for and encourages young women's interest in technology and related careers;
- a mentor–protégé program that matches women with senior members of WIT to create mentoring relationships;
- an annual leadership awards banquet, recognizing women in technology or in affiliated organizations for outstanding leadership;
- special fundraising events to provide philanthropic opportunities for our members and increase the visibility of WIT in the community;

- the Women in Technology Education Foundation, the WIT 501 c (3) charitable foundation dedicated to encouraging and supporting women and girls as they pursue their interests in math, science, and technology;
- publications and listservs that keep members informed of events and news;
- a members-only job bank and a workforce development support group for those who are transitioning between business opportunities;
- strategic alliances with educational, charitable, and other professional organizations to provide growth opportunities for our members and for WIT; and
- long-term, mutually beneficial relationships with corporate sponsors headquartered or with a significant presence in the DC Metro region.

To learn more about WIT and get involved in networking, connecting, learning and interacting with women at all levels in their careers, in all areas of technology, in government and industry, please visit the website (www.womenintechnology.org).

Appendix B

Women in Technology Leadership Awards

The 2009 Leadership Awards marked the tenth anniversary of this prestigious awards program, which recognizes women who have demonstrated leadership in the local technology industry and who exemplify the WIT values of "Connect. Lead. Succeed."

Women leaders are honored in eight categories: corporate, government, entrepreneur, rising star, WIT Champion, WIT President's Award, WIT Founders' Award, and lifetime achievement. For the first time in 2009, WIT also presented a Company Leadership Champion award. This award recognizes companies that consciously develop and advance women into leadership positions.

Award winners are selected by a committee (with the exception of those awards that are made at the President's discretion). The committee consists of a WIT board member; the Leadership Awards chair; a former Leadership Awards winner; a non-WIT executive; and a member of the press/analyst community. Deliberations are kept strictly confidential and are made against an established set of criteria.

Committee operational guidelines and award criteria are listed below.

Committee Operational Guidelines
- Members of the Awards Committee are encouraged to solicit nominations for the awards they will be reviewing or submit nominations on their own. All nominations must be received in writing during the nomination period. Committee members may not submit nominations either verbally or in writing at the selection committee meeting.
- An awards committee judge may not have a nomination submitted on her behalf. If such a nomination has been received, the judge may decide to have the nomination withdrawn or the

judge may choose to step down from the committee so that the nomination may be considered for an award.

- To maintain confidentiality, the Award Committee should conduct its deliberations face-to-face, not in a virtual environment. If a committee member is unable to attend the meeting, the member may submit the scores to the Awards Committee Chair prior to the meeting. Because this committee member will not be participating in the discussions at the meeting, the committee member may not participate in any subsequent votes or scoring of nominations.
- When discussing individual nominations, the committee must limit its discussions to the information presented in the nomination itself. Outside knowledge of a person or program should not be taken into consideration.
- Each award category that the Award Committee reviews specifies a prescribed number of awards. The Award Committee may not change the number of awards given.
- All awards are discretionary. If worthy candidates do not exist, the Awards committee can recommend to the WIT Board that the award not be given in a particular year.

Women in Technology Awards

CORPORATE

- *Purpose:* To honor a woman in a corporate environment who demonstrates exemplary leadership skills.
- *Eligibility:* Any woman who works in industry. She does not need to be a WIT member.
- *Number Given:* One
- *Ideal Candidate:* Any woman who has accelerated and advanced her career beyond typical performance expectations (including work in the community).
- *Selection Criteria:* Candidates will be judged based on their embodiment of the three core WIT values:
  1. Connect
     - Mentoring of others above, below, and at the same level.
     - Developing future leaders in her profession and/or community.
     - Working in the community (evaluated on the candidate's leadership skills and performance, not on the philanthropic nature of what she is doing or contributing).

2. Lead
  * Demonstrated ability to create and implement a vision for her team.
  * Track record of successfully motivating employees and team members.
  * Exhibiting of innovative methods of motivating and mentoring employees and team members.
  * "Pioneering efforts" taken on by the candidate. "Pioneering efforts" do not necessarily have a successful outcome.
3. Succeed
  * Demonstrated success at implementing or promoting technology, management principles, or processes.

GOVERNMENT
* *Purpose:* To honor a woman working for a government agency who demonstrates exemplary leadership skills.
* *Eligibility:* Any woman who works in government. She does not need to be a WIT member.
* *Number Given:* One
* *Ideal Candidate:* Any woman who has accelerated and advanced her career in a government setting.
* *Selection Criteria:* Candidates will be judged based on their embodiment of the three core WIT values:
  1. Connect
    * Mentoring of others above, below, and at the same level.
    * Developing future leaders in her profession and/or community.
  2. Lead
    * Demonstrated ability to create and implement a vision for her team.
    * Track record of successfully motivating employees and team members.
    * Exhibiting of innovative methods of motivating and mentoring employees and team members.
    * "Pioneering efforts" taken on by the candidate. "Pioneering efforts" do not necessarily have a successful outcome.
  3. Succeed
    * Demonstrated success at implementing or promoting technology, management principles, or processes.

ENTREPRENEUR

- *Purpose:* To honor a woman entrepreneur who has demonstrated exemplary leadership traits by starting and operating her own business.
- *Eligibility:* Any woman who works in industry. She does not need to be a WIT member but must own a business that has been in operation for a minimum of two years. Headquarters must be in the Washington Metropolitan area.
- *Number Given:* One
- *Ideal Candidate:* Any woman who has accelerated and advanced her career beyond typical performance expectations (including work in the community).
- *Selection Criteria:* Candidates will be judged based on their embodiment of the three core WIT values:
  1. Connect
     * Mentoring of other individuals and small business owners.
     * Developing future leaders in her profession and/or community.
  2. Lead
     * A trailblazer who has demonstrated her ability to create and implement a vision for her company.
     * Track record of successfully motivating employees and team members.
     * Mentors her staff and contributes to industry, government, and the larger community.
     * "Pioneering efforts" taken on by the candidate. "Pioneering efforts" do not necessarily have a successful outcome.
  3. Succeed
     * Demonstrated success at implementing or promoting technology, management principles, or processes.
     * Has a noteworthy track record in winning business for her company.

RISING STAR

- *Purpose:* To honor a woman, with ten years or less of work experience, who has demonstrated exemplary leadership traits at an early point in her career.
- *Eligibility:* Any woman from government or industry. She does not need to be a member of WIT.
- *Number Given:* One

- *Ideal Candidate:* The ideal candidate is a woman who has distinguished herself from her peers and consistently exceeded performance expectations for their level.
- *Selection Criteria:* In selecting the recipient of this award, the committee should look at how well-rounded the candidate is and how aware she is of the larger community around her. Some things to consider:
  - What has the nominee done to differentiate herself from her peers?
  - Is the nominee a risk taker?
  - Has she participated in the larger IT community around her? If so, how?
  - Has the nominee challenged the status quo?

WIT CHAMPION
- *Purpose*: To honor a current member of WIT who has shown exemplary dedication to the WIT organization and its mission.
- *Eligibility:* A woman who is a member of the WIT community and works in either government or industry.
- *Number Given:* One
- *Ideal Candidate:* The ideal candidate is a woman who has been an active, committed member of WIT for a sustained period of time.
- *Selection Criteria:*
  - Committed to the values of WIT and works to further the organization's mission.
  - Has contributed in a multiple ways throughout different facets of the organization.
  - Takes ownership of and accountability for the projects/roles she takes on, and demonstrates results.
  - Consideration may be given for length of service.

PRESIDENT'S AWARD
- *Purpose:* To allow the WIT President to recognize the WIT member in the current term who has done the most to assist the President in achieving her goals for the WIT year. This can be through outstanding performance in her assigned responsibilities and tasks or for exemplary accomplishment of additional duties "above and beyond" during the year.
- *Eligibility:* Woman who is an active member of the WIT community and works in government or industry.

- *Number Given:* One to two but at the discretion of the WIT President.
- *Selection Criteria:* At the discretion of the WIT President.

FOUNDERS' AWARD
- *Purpose:* To allow the WIT President to recognize and honor a current member of WIT (from either government or industry) who, she believes, has shown exemplary involvement in the WIT organization, and who has demonstrated over time a continued passion for advancing the WIT organization towards its vision.
- *Eligibility:* Woman who is an active member of the WIT community and works in government or industry.
- *Number Given:* One to two but at the discretion of the WIT President.
- *Ideal Candidate:* The candidate is the embodiment of what the Founders envisioned when starting the organization.
- *Selection Criteria:* At the discretion of the WIT President.

LIFETIME ACHIEVEMENT AWARD
- *Purpose:* To recognize an outstanding individual for extraordinary, long-term contributions and role modeling to the IT community over a significant period of time.
- *Eligibility:* Award is given to one of the nominees in the corporate, entrepreneur, or government categories. Rising Star nominees are not eligible.
- *Number Given:* One (This award does not need to be given each year. It should be reserved for a truly extraordinary contributor to the organization.)
- *Ideal Candidate:* Any woman who has met the criteria for the corporate, government, or entrepreneur award but who also has a significant track record of long-term, extraordinary contributions to the IT community over a significant period of time throughout her career.
- *Selection Criteria:*
  - Delivers on commitments.
  - Serves as a mentor in her professional career.
  - Embodies a selfless attitude in all matters.
  - Outstanding role model who has achieved a measure of success in her professional career yet consistently supports the advancement of women around her.

COMPANY LEADERSHIP AWARD

- *Purpose:* To recognize technology companies that support and advance women into leadership positions.
- *Eligibility:* For details, please see Appendix D. To inquire about the application process, please contact staff@womenintechnology.org

Information on upcoming Awards programs and calls for nominations are typically posted to the WIT website (www.womenintechnology.org) in January or February of any given year. Please check the website at that time to nominate a candidate for a future award. For a comprehensive list of award winners, 2000–2009, please see Appendix C.

Appendix C

WIT Award Winners: An Exceptional List of Extraordinary Women

2009

Corporate: Jeanne O'Kelley, Senior Vice President and General Manager, Vangent

Government: Susan Keen, Technical Director, Navy Enterprise Resource Planning Program Department of the Navy

Entrepreneur: Kelly Harman, President, Zephyr Strategy

Rising Star: Glenda Morgan, Ph.D., Director of Technology and Learning Initiatives, George Mason University

WIT Champion: Gayle Sweeney, Principal, North Highland Group

President's Award: Charlotte Pelliccia, President, Pelliccia Communications

Founders' Award: Louise Peabody, Partner, Watkins, Meegan, Drury & Co.

Lifetime Achievement: Debra McKeldin, Chief Enterprise Architect/ Deputy Director, Centers for Medicare and Medicaid Services, Enterprise Architecture Strategy Group, Office of Information Services

Company Leadership Champion Award: HP and SAP

2008

Corporate: Tami A. Erwin, President, Washington/Baltimore/ Virginia Region, Verizon Wireless

Government: Laurie Reyes, Police Officer 3/Project Lifesaver Coordinator, Montgomery County Department of Police

Entrepreneur: Katie Sleep, President and CEO, List Innovative Solutions

Rising Star: Nikole Collins-Puri, Global Business Services Diversity and Inclusion Manager, AT&T

WIT Champion: Carol Moroz, Client Services Executive, SAP

President's Award: Kathryn Harris, Principal and Founder, Resolution Law Group

Founders' Award: Marguerete Luter, President, The Process Pro

Lifetime Achievement: Deirdre Murray, Business Development Principal, Qwest Government Services, Inc.

2007

Corporate: Deborah Alderson, President, System and Network Solutions Group, SAIC

Government: Dr. Janice Cuny, Director, Information Technology, National Science Foundation

Entrepreneur: Rose Wang, CEO, Binary Group

Rising Star: Jennifer Murrill, Operations Researcher/Cost Analyst, Northrop Grumman Information Technology

WIT Champion: Ardell Fleeson, Managing Director, Business Development, Human Capital Advisors, LLC

President's Award: Charlotte Pelliccia, President, Pelliccia Communications

Founders' Award: Eva Neumann, President, ENC Marketing, Inc.

2006

Corporate: Barbara Anderson, Vice President, State & Local Government, EDS

Government: Karyn Hayes-Ryan, Deputy Director, Acquisition Engineering/Program Manager, Engineering Enterprise, National Geospatial-Intelligence Agency

Entrepreneur: Debra Ruh, President and CEO, TecAccess

Rising Star: Leah Hooten-Clark, Senior Electronics Engineer, Northrop Grumman

WIT Champion: Charlotte Pelliccia, President, Pelliccia Communications

President's Award: Kathy Albarado, President, Helios HR, and Toni Townes, Vice President and Partner, Unisys

Founders' Award: Dede Haskins, Vice President of Marketing and Training and Managing Principal, Cigital

2005

Corporate: Catherine Szpindor, Vice President of IT Enterprise Services, Nextel Communications

Government: Captain Anne-marie Hartlaub, Director, Organization and Management Services Division, U.S. Navy

Entrepreneur: Elizabeth Shea, Co-Founder and Principal, SheaHedges Group, LLC

Rising Star: Jennifer Bleier, Assistant Deputy Program Manager for the Industrial Computer Security Program, SAIC

WIT Champion: Marla Ozarowski, Director of Technology Adoption, Freddie Mac

President's Award: Sandy Scearce, Director of Business Development, Grant Thornton

Founders' Award: Angela Drummond, President and CEO, SiloSmashers

Lifetime Achievement: Lydia Thomas, President and CEO, Mitretek Systems

2004

Corporate: Linda Keene Solomon, Partner, Deloitte Consulting LLP

Government: Linda Jacksta, Director, Systems Engineering, U.S. Bureau of Customs and Border Protection

Entrepreneur: Sandra K. Richardson, Co-Founder and Chief Operating Officer, Métier, Ltd.

Rising Star: Amy Bielski, Vice President, Web & Technology Solutions Group, Social & Health Services Division, ORC Macro

WIT Champion: Ellen Quinn, Quality Assurance Manager, Northrop Grumman Information Technology

President's Award: Debbie Thacker, Executive Vice President, BTL Services, Inc.

Founders' Award: Deanne Inman, Director, Deloitte & Touche LLP

2003

Corporate: Vonya McCann, Senior Vice President, Federal External Affairs, Sprint

Government: Deborah Loudon, Deputy CIO, National Reconnaissance Office

Entrepreneur: Kimberly McCabe, President and CEO, Advanced Performance Consulting Group, Inc.

WIT Champion: Marguerete Luter, Vice President, Global Bid Management, Unisys Global Network

President's Award: Amy Lemon, Controller, Financial Planning and Analysis, Vastera, Inc. and Sally Turner, Director, Business Development, Federal Solutions, AMS

Founders' Award: Mary Wall Dale, Client Relationship Executive, Unisys

Lifetime Achievement: Vivien Crea, Rear Admiral, United States Coast Guard

2002

Corporate: Linda Gooden, President, Information Technology, Lockheed Martin, and Donna Morea, Executive Vice President, AMS

Government: Miriam Browning, Office of the Army Chief Information Officer, Office of the Secretary of the Army, United States Army, and Joan R. Vallancewhitacre, Executive Officer, Information Services, National Imagery and Mapping Agency (NIMA)

Entrepreneur: Corinna E. Lathan, Ph.D., President and CEO, AnthroTronix, Inc., and Dr. Helena S. Wisniewski, Chairman and CEO, Aurora Biometrics, Inc.

President's Award: Lisa Throckmorton, Account Manager, The SheaHedges Group, and Dede Haskins, Vice President of Operations, EastBanc Technologies, LLC (Alazar, LLC)

Founders' Award: Betty Arbuckle, Partner, Washington Financial Group, LLP

Lifetime Achievement: Faith Driscoll, Patent Attorney, Bull HN Information Systems

2001

Leadership: Paula Jagemann, President and CEO, eCommerce Industries Inc.; Ginger Ehn Lew, CEO and Managing Director, TDF-Telecommunications Development Fund; and TiTi McNeill, President and CEO, TranTech, Inc.

President's Award: Ana Maria Boitel, Director of Business Development, OP•X, and Eva Neumann, President, ENC Marketing, Inc.

Founders' Award: Deirdre Murray, Group Manager, Market Development, Sprint Government Systems Division

Lifetime Achievement: Esther Thomas Smith, Partner, Qorvis Communications

2000

President's Award: Eva Neumann, President, ENC Marketing, Inc.

Appendix D

Women in Technology Company Leadership Award

Women in Technology created the Company Leadership Award to recognize technology companies that support and advance women into leadership positions. In May 2009, after a fifteen-month review process, Hewlett Packard (HP) and Systems Applications and Products in Data Processing (SAP) were the first two companies to receive the WIT Company Leadership Award.

HP

Chris Alexander, Human Resources Manager, Diversity
Tom Hempfield, Vice President and General Manager, U.S. Federal

HP continued to retain and advance women at all levels of the organization over the past year by implementing a number of key initiatives in its Technology Solutions Group Americas Division (TSGA).

Recognized as a best practice, HP's Talent Management Program focused discussions with senior management on key talent, with diversity as a priority. HP has established metrics for recruiting women and presenting a diverse set of candidates for all vacancies at all levels. Board Members of the TSGA Women's Board nominated high-potential females for mentor relationships while supporting a growing Women's Network.

HP continues to educate, promote, and sustain awareness for the importance of diversity, which is no longer just an HR initiative but is seen as critical to the company's business success. Women now occupy thirty percent of senior management positions in four key businesses within TSGA, and HP is establishing an aggressive fifty percent goal for women in senior management across the board for 2010 to further the division's commitment to gender diversity.

SAP
Alice Leong, Vice President of Global Diversity

In 2008, SAP worked to support and advance women at all levels of its global workforce and to maintain the percentage of women in senior management positions in the U.S. at roughly thirty percent overall.

Over the past year, SAP launched an education and awareness campaign for its senior leadership to give women within the company better and more visible support and sponsorship. The company also continued to integrate awareness of its diversity efforts into its manager on-boarding agenda. In 2009, for example, SAP is establishing Key Performance Indicators at the senior management levels to identify and track the careers of high-potential women in the company.

Efforts to remove inadvertent bias in the annual talent review process aim to ensure better representation of women in the pool of top talent and high-potential employees. In North America, the Business Women's Network at SAP grew from twenty-two participants to almost 300, providing visible leadership sponsorship, mentoring, and learning opportunities to women at all levels.

Appendix E

WIT Boards of Directors

2009–2010

EXECUTIVE COMMITTEE

President: Toni Townes-Whitley, VP & Managing Partner, North America, Unisys Global Industries

President-Elect: Nanci Schimizzi, VP Technology, FINRA

Secretary: Jean Leonard, Group Vice President Business Development, QinetiQ

Treasurer: Cynthia Sanchez, Director of Financial Planning and Analysis, ContourGlobal, Inc.

General Counsel: Kathryn Harris, Principal, The Resolution Law Group, PLC

BOARD MEMBERS AT LARGE

Immediate Past President: Sue Liblong, Vice President, Marketing and Business Development, SiloSmashers

Member Development: Rose Wang, CEO, Binary Group

SIG Liaison: Mary Ann Wagner, Principal, XIO Strategies

Special Events: Patricia Burke, Principal, SRA International

Strategic Alliances: Lisa Dezzutti, President, Market Connections, Inc.

Women in Government: Mary Davie, Assistant Commissioner, GSA/ Federal Acquisition Service

ELECTED COMMITTEE CHAIRS

Communications: Liz Anthony, Federal Channels Marketing Manager, Cisco

Programs: Kelly Harman, President and Owner, Zephyr Strategy

Membership: Piper Conrad, Senior Director, SpeakerBox Communications

Sponsorship: Nancy Lamberton, Founding Partner, Excitations, LLC

EXECUTIVE COMMITTEE
President: Sue Liblong, Vice President, Marketing and Business
    Development, SiloSmashers
President-Elect: Toni Townes-Whitley, VP & Managing Partner,
    North America Unisys Global Industries
Treasurer: Raluca Monet, Strategic Business Operations Manager,
    Unisys
Secretary: Jean Leonard, Group Vice President Operations &
    Business Development, QinetiQ
General Counsel: Kathryn Harris, Principal, The Resolution Law
    Group, PLC

BOARD MEMBERS AT LARGE
Immediate Past President: Charlotte Pelliccia, President, Pelliccia
    Communications
Member Development: Rose Wang, CEO, Binary Group
SIG Liaison: Gayle Sweeney, Principal, North Highland Company
Special Events: Patricia Burke, Project Manager, Federal Acquisition
    Institute Support Team, SRA
Strategic Alliances: Lisa Dezzutti, President, Market Connections, Inc.
Women in Government: Linda Y. Cureton, Chief Information
    Officer, NASA Goddard Space Flight Center

ELECTED COMMITTEE CHAIRS
Communications: Liz Anthony, Federal Channels Marketing
    Manager, Cisco
Programs: Kelly Harman, President and Owner, Zephyr Strategy
Membership: Nanci Schimizzi, Vice President Technology and
    Chief of Staff, FINRA
Sponsorship: Jennifer Hooker, Executive Recruiter, Booz Allen
    Hamilton

Appendix F

The Women in Technology Education Foundation (WITEF)

The Women in Technology Education Foundation is WIT's 501c(3) charitable foundation dedicated to encouraging and supporting women and girls as they pursue their interests in math, science, engineering and technology. WITEF's goal is to increase the number of girls who will choose these fields for their future education and careers, particularly girls in underserved communities.

WITEF creates awareness and support for this goal by providing funding for education, mentoring, and training programs and by awarding scholarships and grants to nonprofit organizations and individual women and girls.

Unless exposed at a very early age to the practices of mathematics, the sciences, engineering, and technology in general, many girls will lag behind their male counterparts in not only their school-aged years, but also in their ensuing professional careers. Therefore, WITEF believes it is critical to empower young girls by engaging them in technology and computer-related learning during their elementary, middle, and high school years.

WITEF has helped hundreds of girls in local communities by providing mentors and speakers, as well as financial support, for field trips; assisting with program and curriculum development; providing program resources for Career Days in Virginia, Maryland, and Washington, D.C.; and exploring any and all opportunities to expose girls to technology.

WITEF's efforts are helping ensure that the next generation of professional women is well equipped for tomorrow's challenges.

Appendix G

Contributors

Foreword

Maureen Bunyan serves as Prime News Anchor WJLA-TV (ABC 7) and has won seven local Emmys for her work. Founder of the International Women's Media and of the National Association of Black Journalists, Ms. Bunyan has been inducted into the Hall of Fame of the Washington Chapter of the Society of Professional Journalists and The Silver Circle of the National Academy of Television Arts and Sciences.

Stories

Kathy Albarado is CEO of Helios HR, a human resources consulting and outsourcing firm.

Dianne Black is an information technology executive specializing in the Internet and telecommunications industries.

Althea Blackwell is self-proclaimed "geekette" who writes about government technology and produces a cable show and YouTube channel about technology.

Marnie Bloom is an executive leadership coach and management consultant.

Page Bostic is a director at Marriott International, Inc., and a certified Project Management Professional (PMP) who has a passion for developing others.

Madelyn Clark-Robinson is an executive coach working with corporate, not-for-profit and government leaders in designing and implementing changes that make them and their organizations most effective.

Piper Conrad provides marketing communications counsel to technology companies.

Patricia A. Crew is a licensed, clinical counselor providing career consulting services to a broad range of upwardly mobile professionals.

Susan Filocco is an independent business process consultant and an energetic volunteer for children's causes and the environment.

Kathy Furlong is Director of Business Development Operations at Nortel Government Solutions.

Cathy Hubbs is a champion for safeguarding the confidentiality, integrity, and availability of digital data in higher education.

Pam Krulitz is an executive coach specializing in working with technology leaders.

Cindy Lancaster is a capture and proposal professional who is inspired to greatness by the stories of the amazing women in this book.

Rebecca L. Mann recruits professionals for international development projects.

Lachelle McMillan is an independent consultant focused on program management and business information systems and processes.

Raluca Monet is a strategic business operations lead at Unisys Corporation.

Martha J. Padgette is an engineer with Northrop Grumman, providing UNIX System Administration, Oracle DBA and Web application support to U.S. Government customers for large database systems.

Loyce Best Pailen is an educator, technologist, and administrator advancing the distance learning space at University of Maryland University College.

Ellen Quinn is an ASQ certified Manager of Quality and Organizational Excellence who inspires process improvement through teamwork.

Nancy Rawles is an HR executive who delights in learning about leadership and bringing that learning to the organization she serves.

Maria Sanders is a director of recruiting at Resources Global, a professional services firm.

Anne Teehan is a certified leadership coach and business consultant with a passion for helping others learn and succeed.

Paula Tarnapol Whitacre is principal of Full Circle Communications, LLC, a writing and editing firm based in Alexandria.

Steering Committee
Chair: Charlotte Pelliccia
Members: Joanne Lozar Glenn, Marguerete Luter, Kim Sanz

Interviewing
Chair: Pam Krulitz
Members: Kathy Albarado, Dianne Black, Althea Blackwell, Marnie I. Bloom, Page Bostic, Madelyn Clark-Robinson, Piper Conrad, Patricia A Crew, Susan Filocco, Kathy Furlong, Bette George, Cathy Hubbs, Cindy Lancaster, Rebecca Mann, Lachelle McMillan, Raluca Monet, Martha J. Padgette, Loyce Best Pailen, Ellen C. Quinn, Nancy Rawles, Maria Sanders, Anne Teehan, Paula Tarnapol Whitacre

Editing
Chair: Joanne Lozar Glenn
Members: Leigh Albert, Mary Chapman, Marcia J. Drucker, Cathy Hubbs, Carol A. Montoya, Martha J. Padgette, Robyn Rickenbach, Jane Tam

Publishing
Chair: Valerie Voci
Members: Christine Dobday, Susan Filocco, Joanne Lozar Glenn, Raluca Monet

Marketing
Co-Chairs: Penelope Parker and Charlotte Pelliccia
Members: Robin Bectel, Lori Boerner, Page Bostic, Lynne Brodie, Christine Chen, Piper Conrad, Patricia Harris, Rebecca Mann, Sapna Mehra, Deanna Nelson, Leila Mathur Peck, Nancy Rollman, Brenda Seldin, Barbara Sweet, Sonya Starnes, Jane Tam

Made in the USA